# A Carolina Plantation
## Remembered

Line drawing of Friendfield Plantation by Ray Govus, 1980. *Postcard collection, courtesy of Ed Carter.*

# IN THOSE DAYS

# A Carolina Plantation
## Remembered

Frances Cheston Train

THE
History
PRESS

Published by The History Press
Charleston, SC  29403
www.historypress.net

First published 2008

ISBN 978.1.540229212

Library of Congress Cataloging-in-Publication Data

Train, Frances Cheston.
A Carolina plantation remembered : in those days / Frances Cheston Train.
p. cm.

1.  Train, Frances Cheston--Childhood and youth. 2.  Train, Frances
Cheston--Homes and haunts--South Carolina--Georgetown. 3.
Plantations--South Carolina--Georgetown--History--20th century. 4.
Plantation life--South Carolina--Georgetown--History--20th century. 5.
Georgetown (S.C.)--Social life and customs--20th century. 6.  Georgetown
(S.C.)--Biography.  I. Title.
F279.G3T73 2007
975.7'89--dc22
[B]
2007041048

This memoir is for the dear memory of my mother and father; my sisters and brothers; my widely extended family then and now; my husband John; my children Alix, Whitney, Frances and Harry; my grandchildren Josiah, Will, Chessie, Thomas, Whitney III and Harry Jr.; and to the memory of my devoted nurse, Margaret.

*As for you few remaining friends*
*You are dearer to me every day.*
*How short the road became*
*That seemed to be so long.*
—Anna Akhmatova

# Contents

# Acknowledgements

Without constant coaching in the mysteries of word processing by my expert and patient teachers, Tom Tutor, Jim Mayers and Sonia Dobson, I would not have been able to compose these happy memories. The Furman Printers in Bedford Hills saw me through many versions, with special thanks to Paula Kornbrust. Many thanks to my South Carolina friends: Virginia McClary for her wonderful reminiscences; Debbie Summey for her patient and expert research; Dale Rosengarten, curator of Special Collections at the College of Charleston Library; Lee Brockington of the Baruch Foundation; David Drayton for his knowledge of Black History; and Ed Carter for his marvelous postcard collection. My editor Mark Donovan pulled the scattered vignettes into shape, and I was greatly encouraged by Melissa Schwefel of The History Press and by my many friends who understand life "In Those Days." Thank you.

.

# CHAPTER 1

# Overnight to South Carolina

Every evening we could hear the long wailing whistle of the Black Diamond freight train warning of its approach to the crossing near our house in Whitemarsh, Pennsylvania. Sometimes I would stand by the edge of the creek and look at the cars silhouetted against the western sky as they rattled over the high trestle bridge. The setting sun beamed between the wheels, the steamy smoke smelled of cinders and the earth trembled under my shoes. The engineer, wearing his jaunty black-and-white striped railroad cap, piloted the mighty locomotive with one hand, his elbow resting casually on the ledge of the cab. I would wave, and he'd grin and wave back. One day he blew two more blasts on the whistle just for me, and I wished with all my heart that I could go with him.

At that time, in the early 1930s, I thought every train, even the freights, went to Maine or to South Carolina, the two places to which my family traveled regularly. Every year my anticipation would build up to a fit of the jitters by the time the day of departure finally arrived.

My mother, father, Marg, my nurse, and our two shivering dogs waited next to the heaps of bags on a gritty, cold platform of Philadelphia's 30th Street Station. The train always seemed to be late. At last the brilliant searchlight flicked back and forth far down the track, and the announcement boomed and echoed through the station: "The Palmetto, arriving on Track 2. Train for Wilmington! Baltimore! Washington! Richmond! And points south! ALLLL ABOARRRRRRD!"

The long train, with its brakes hissing and steaming and its bell clanging, drew past the clumps of waiting passengers. White-jacketed porters leaned out to welcome them and assist the redcaps with the baggage. We hurried to find the right rooms—Drawing Room A and Compartment B. No sooner were we settled when the train eased out of the station, and we were on our way at last!

Typical cabins on the street in the 1930s. *Courtesy of Frances Cheston Train.*

Train travel in those days was wonderful fun for children, completely different from being a passive, buckled up captive in an airplane. There was so much to do and observe. Our compartment—containing my nurse, me and Duggie, my Scottie—connected with the drawing room where my parents were ensconced with Trigger, their huge, smelly springer spaniel, stacks of Louis Vuitton luggage and English shotguns in polished leather cases. The redcaps piled all the duffels and extra bags in the vestibule between the cars. No one ever worried about theft on the overnight trip.

One thing that did worry me, though, was what would happen if my dog made a "mistake" on the dark green carpet. I was certain that the all-powerful conductor would throw me off the train—a fate too awful to contemplate. I imagined how terrible it would be for a seven-year-old in blue flannel pajamas to be left behind on some cold, windy platform, and I dreaded the conductor's buzz at the door. He would check the folder of tickets, punch them efficiently, hand the copies off to his sidekick and then glare enigmatically at the dog. What was he thinking?

So, I would get off at Wilmington, the next stop, and drag my poor dog by his unaccustomed leash, his toenails scraping on the inhospitable cement, and beg him to go. He never would, although he encouraged me with interminable, prolonged, disdainful sniffs. He preferred grass and bushes, and he clearly made up his stubborn Scottie mind that railroad platforms were not for that purpose. I feared his delaying tactics would cause us to

Lafayette Bridge. Georgetown, South Carolina. *Postcard collection, courtesy of Ed Carter.*

miss the train, and I had to run to get on board, filled with misgivings and mission unaccomplished. In spite of my anxiety, somehow he always lasted until morning.

I loved our cozy, tan-painted room with its varnished trim and the green plush seats with snowy linen antimacassars buttoned to their backs, but once the bags were stowed and the dogs admonished to "Be good!" I couldn't wait to rush out into the swaying passageway. Following the signs that read "Dining Car in the Rear," I ran ahead of Marg, bouncing off the walls of the corridors, exaggerating the jerkiness of the train on purpose. I skipped daringly across the shifting plates between the cars like Eliza crossing the ice in *Uncle Tom's Cabin*, engulfed by the train's scary, deafening rattle and the cold, cindery wind until I reached the safety of the next car.

It was fun to peek into other people's compartments on the way. I watched red-faced, tweedy gentlemen swirling clear chunks of ice in tall whiskey glasses and their wives—blue-haired and stiffly corseted—playing cards or drinking cocktails poured from their own frosted silver shakers. It was almost the end of Prohibition, but I was unaware they were breaking any laws. In those days, everyone dressed formally for train travel, the gentlemen wearing three-piece suits and ties, and the ladies sporting hats and traveling suits with jeweled lapel pins and pearls.

Some of them had children, whom I examined suspiciously and who looked just as strange to me as I must have to them. I prayed that my family

River scene. Georgetown, South Carolina. *Postcard collection, courtesy of Ed Carter.*

wouldn't know any of them for fear we would have to be introduced, but unfortunately they usually did. The people in the Pullmans in those days constituted a sort of a club—those who were going to shoot in South Carolina and Georgia and the more richly-dressed "Others" who were traveling to Palm Beach. I never wondered why my family knew so many of the other passengers, and it never crossed my mind that we were in any way privileged.

After the drawing room and the compartments came the sections in the regular Pullman car. To transform it into a sleeper, the porter would pull out the seats and fit them together, haul down the upper and make up the berths. Each individual section was then partitioned from the aisle by two green curtains of a heavy, impenetrable baize material, which the occupant, once safely inside, buttoned tightly together. When big people attempted to undress in their berths, the curtains bulged and billowed alarmingly, and it was tempting to give the bulge a fast slap or pinch while dashing by.

I lurched through the coaches where whole families would be preparing for the long night of sitting up. Babies slept in their mothers' laps, and weary older folk stared out the window. Messy newspapers were crumpled under the seats, and the smell of orange peel and fried chicken pervaded the atmosphere. The older kids stared at me guardedly. I knew I looked

River scene. Georgetown, South Carolina. *Postcard collection, courtesy of Ed Carter.*

alien in my gray flannel skirt and Buster Brown oxfords as I trotted through on my way to the dining car.

The club car was filled with noisy men playing cards. I always ran as fast as possible through the smoke and sour, heavy smell of liquor to the first part of the diner, the corridor by the galley, where I joined the line of people in its passageway waiting to be seated by the steward. I looked out the window at the rows of houses that edged the tracks. They were so close as we rattled by that I could spy into their kitchens and see the wallpaper patterns. I thought about those children listening to their favorite radio programs while doing their homework. It was like inventing families for a dollhouse.

As soon as the steward showed us to the table, the waiter dexterously arranged a full complement of heavy silver flatware beside each place after selecting them individually from a pile underneath the big window. There was always a long-stemmed rose or carnation jiggling in the brightly polished bud vase on every table. The linen napkins were heavily starched and immaculately folded. It made me feel important to write my own order. The waiter smiled patiently as if he had all the time in the world balancing there in his ankle-length white apron as I painstakingly printed each choice. He studied it with care before ripping off the first sheet, leaving the carbon for the head steward to add up with great flourishes of his pencil when it came time for my father to pay.

Front Street. Georgetown, South Carolina. *Postcard collection, courtesy of Ed Carter.*

The cooks and waiters on the Pullman trains were always colored, but in those days the steward was a white man. I noticed that the shoulders of his blue serge uniform were sprinkled with dandruff, and he seemed preoccupied and not very kind to the jolly waiters. When he made change, he peeled the singles off a fat roll of bills and set down each coin with a little thump on a small silver tray.

The perspiring cooks turned out a variety of delicious dishes from the crowded little kitchen. They wore starched white tunics and tall chef's hats and did all the cooking to order on a sizzling coal-burning range. When the cooks finished preparing the meals, a waiter loaded the dinners onto a huge tin tray, which he balanced on the upturned palm of one hand, and made his way back to the table, swaying gracefully with the roll and lurch of the train.

The waiter placed each thick plate precisely in front of the diner before removing its heavy chrome dome with a flourish. He always remembered who ordered what, and the dinner arrived in jig time—choices of soup, fried chicken, grilled steak or fried fish. Dessert was flaky crusted apple cherry pie à la mode or vanilla ice cream with hot chocolate sauce served in frosty chrome compotes. Afterwards the waiter gave us silver-chrome finger bowls lined with fluted paper. And all the while, the changing scene scrolled by—towns, bridges, rivers, factories and houses—passing images seen and recorded through the clear, clean windows of childhood, the memories preserved for a lifetime.

High Market Street. Georgetown, South Carolina. *Postcard collection, courtesy of Ed Carter.*

Each Pullman car had its own evocative name. By the time we got back to our sleeping car, passing through Savannah River, Island Home, Rice Bird and others, our porter would be making up the berths. Reaching way up, his white jacket hiked high over tight, shiny black trousers, standing on tiptoe in his polished black boots he let down the khaki-colored upper berth using a special lug wrench he unsnapped from its place by the small rotating fan near the ceiling. He shrugged the pillows into their cases with a snap, hooked up the little ladder and then buttoned on the green webbing that was supposed to keep the occupant of the top bunk from falling out. This turned out to be just the thing for playing Tarzan. In the upper berth, I'd stick my arms and legs through the gaps while he made up the lower, joking and storytelling all the while, ducking his head good-naturedly to avoid my swinging feet.

First he tucked the snowy bottom sheet snugly over the mattress, then a top sheet, two tan and yellow patterned blankets with PULLMAN CO. woven into the wool and a third sheet over that for a blanket cover. He rolled a spare blanket into a tight cylinder under the window, plumped up the pillows and finally turned down the bed in an inviting fold. All this took about ten minutes. Finally, the porter wrote down our destination for the morning wake-up call and reminded us to leave our shoes in the little two-way hinged compartment if we wanted them polished during the night.

In the bathroom there was fresh ice water in the thermos jug in its bracket near the round, gleaming stainless steel sink and a holder

Old Market and Town Hall, rebuilt in 1842. The present structure is an exact brick replica of the old wooden structure that was destroyed in the hurricane of 1822. *Postcard collection, courtesy of Ed Carter.*

Broad Street with Confederate Monument and St. Mary's Catholic Church. *Postcard collection, courtesy of Ed Carter.*

filled with elegant paper-cone cups. A sign over the toilet contained a memorable warning, and all of us children sang its words to the melody of Dvorak's *Humoresque*:

> *Passengers Will Please Refrain*
> *From Flushing Toilet When The Train*
> *Is Standing In The Station*

When you flushed, you got a strong whiff of cinders, a blast of cold air on your bottom, and—through the open flap in the bowl—a mysterious glimpse of the gravelly railroad bed noisily zipping by underneath.

Better not to wonder what happened to what you did. The grown-ups would never discuss it anyway. They were odd about toilets. My mother always admonished me to use one of the slippery tissue paper seat covers she brought with her on trips, or else to arrange little segments of toilet paper around the seat. They always slipped off before I sat down, and I didn't see the point of them anyway.

Later, in my lower berth, swaying in the clicketyclacking dark after Marg went to sleep in the upper, I pinched the brass catch and moved the dark green shade. Propped up on the high pillows, I watched the land rocket by under the starlight.

19

Presbyterian Church. Georgetown, South Carolina. *Postcard collection, courtesy of Ed Carter.*

I always tried to stay awake at least until Washington where I would see the wondrous sight of the great floodlit Capitol Dome and the luminous obelisk of the Washington Monument floating in the black skyline like the magic Emerald City of Oz. After that, sleep would overcome me until I was jolted awake at Richmond. There the train switched tracks and joined the Atlantic Coastline system, jerking, hissing and clanging as it whizzed and creaked backwards, the apparently random maneuvers ending with a crash as it coupled on a new dining car or changed engines.

Robert Benchley once wrote that whenever he took the sleeper train south he was sure the engineer allowed his eight-year-old nephew to practice driving the engine in the middle of the night, and that's exactly how it felt! I hurriedly yanked down the shade when the train pulled into the station for fear someone would look in the window and see me in bed in my pajamas. Lying on my stomach, squinting through the crack at the very bottom of the blind, I spied on the brawny workers towing long, heavy carts piled high with gray mail sacks and passengers hurrying for the train. Far down the track I watched the brakeman signaling with a lantern.

These were the days of the Depression, and it is hard for me to believe now that I was not aware of class or poverty or that people might resent a small, rich person lying there in the Pullman sleeper when so many other children were sitting up uncomfortably all night long in the coaches.

Duncan Memorial Methodist Church. Georgetown, South Carolina. *Postcard collection, courtesy of Ed Carter.*

At first light, I raised the shade again and with a thrill gazed out over a totally changed landscape: the South, so completely different from home. The train now jiggled comfortably over flat sandy soil, past tall, narrow tobacco-drying sheds and acres of longleaf and loblolly pine. In just one night we left behind factories and cities and rolling pastures and winter-bare woodlands. The colors changed to shades of washed-out beige contrasting with the soft green of the pines. The morning light flooded over fallow fields of tawny broom sedge and pale gold stubble in the cornfields. Gray cypress trees with hanks of Spanish moss caught limply in their spindly branches stood in swamp water that gleamed black as ink.

The land was unfenced and the crossings were without signals except for the warning whistle of the train. The engine often killed cattle that grazed between the rails, and trucks and jalopies frequently stalled on the tracks. It was a rare trip when something wasn't hit. When the train stopped, the passengers got out and stared at the accident.

Masonic Temple and former Colonial Banking House, built in 1735. Georgetown, South Carolina. *Postcard collection, courtesy of Ed Carter.*

Because of these hazards our progress slowed once we reached the Carolinas, leaving time to absorb the intimate details of the familiar Southern landscape as we steamed close by unpainted or whitewashed cabins set off the ground on shaky brick columns. Dark pine smoke spiraled from their leaning chimneys and drifted into the blue Carolina sky. Typically, a black three-legged iron pot for washing clothes sat out front in the yard, and whitewashed automobile tires lined the path to the cabin. A few scrawny chickens and a big old rooster might be pecking in the dust beside the rickety pigpen leaning precariously against a gum tree. Inside the pen, lean black hogs waited for breakfast, their wet pink noses snuffling against the boards.

I saw two women sitting on the front steps of their cabin smoking clay pipes. Their little girls, hair braided into spiky pigtails, skipped about and waved at the passing train. A boy in faded denim bib overalls hung around, solemn and shy, and skinny hound dogs gazed out mournfully from under the porch. Out in the field a farmer leaned on the handles of his plow, turning over the earth for an early crop of collards or tobacco, his mule plodding steadily onward, ears wagging, head down. Another day was beginning.

The train crept right through the center of the towns, which all seemed alike with wide, empty streets fronted by one- and two-story buildings. There were loan offices, pawnbrokers, department stores, five-and-tens, the corner bank, the feed and grain store, the ornate movie theater, many churches and usually a courthouse with an imposing pillared portico. This was a land where the white sheriff's word imposed the Law, the Baptist and African Methodist Episcopal churches furnished hope and comfort and signs labeled public toilets as Men, Women and "Colored."

Our destination, Kingstree, was a flag stop on the Atlantic Coastline Railroad. It was named after the immensely tall longleaf pines that the British preferred for the masts of Royal Navy ships in the eighteenth century. Scattered remnants are still found in the forests today, and the pines are even more valuable because of their scarcity.

We had arrived! Our sixteen bags, the gun cases and the frantic dogs—bursting with excitement and other things—were safely set out on the wooden platform that stretched between long tobacco sheds and storehouses filled with overstuffed bales of cotton. As I walked onto the platform, I was surprised to feel the balmy air on my skin after the dank chill of the North.

My father tipped the porter about two dollars for his uncomplaining work, and he bowed and ducked his head, smiling his extravagant thank-yous—astonished and grateful, or so he wanted us to believe. After picking up the little yellow stool he had set out to aid us in dismounting, he leaned way out from the Pullman car and waved goodbye to us with his cap, his white jacket reflecting the sunlight as the train dwindled away, clacking on down to Georgia. The men from our plantation were always there to meet us. I can still hear their soft Gullah accents, their jokes and affectionate happy greetings. I loved them all, and their welcome lives on in my heart.

After the overnight train ride from Philadelphia, we had a fifty-mile drive from the railroad station at Kingstree to our plantation in Georgetown, South Carolina. On the flat, two-lane highway bordered by featureless pine forest and small pastures, the trip seemed to take an eternity.

The ride was made a little shorter for me by the comical stories told by Pat McClary, longtime manager of our family's plantation and every child's best friend. Pat had a thick Southern accent and was fluent in the local Gullah dialect, and he delighted us with a never-ending repertoire of jokes and funny tales. He was a large man, big of girth and big of heart, who lived for hunting and shooting, family and country and for the care of Friendfield Plantation. He would remain there as resident manager for forty-two years, from 1930 to 1972, and he was a grandfather figure to me, and later to my own children. Bouncing along in the back of his pickup truck, speeding on the rutted dirt roads of the plantation and spotting game—possums, coons, deer, owls, hawks or (heaven forbid) stray cats—was our idea of happiness.

The truck would lurch to a halt, *CRACK!* went the .22 rifle and before our horrified eyes a cat met its demise. (Pat believed they ate the quail eggs and couldn't be tolerated—they were just another predator.) This may sound cruel, but in those days shotguns, rifles and hunting were an everyday part of my world.

Once on that long drive home from Kingstree, Pat told me a disturbing story. I was just a little girl and never questioned local customs—I accepted the system as "just the way things were." He told me about the time a cow crossed over from her unfenced pasture onto Highway 526 and was killed by our pickup. It could have caused a nasty accident, but there was little damage to truck or passengers. Pat told James, the driver, to load up the dead cow onto the truck, take her back to the kennel and "feed her to de dawgs."

Farmers had no rights because their land was unfenced, loose livestock wandered pretty much at their own risk and roadkill was fair game on a public highway. I felt sad for the farmer and sorry for the cow. A first glimmering of rural Southern attitudes began to dawn on me, and I doubt the farmer—who was probably a black sharecropper or a "po' white buckra"—was notified or compensated.

# CHAPTER 2

# Friendfield Plantation: The History

James Withers, Friendfield Plantation's first owner, purchased the core lands in 1734 and early on became a wealthy indigo planter, then a brick maker in Charles Town and rice planter along the Sampit River. In the early eighteenth century the British colony of Carolina was "considered an offshoot of Barbados." It is thought that Withers emigrated from Barbados where many of the British settlers were already engaged in the planting of rice. The slaves who accompanied his family to South Carolina were experienced in the methods and knowledge of wet-field rice cultivation from their past heritage in West Africa—probably today's Sierra Leone and Senegal. Without their expertise, the enormous success of the many rice growing plantations in the area near Georgetown would never have been possible. There were forty-four rice plantations along the Waccamaw River alone, and many others fronting the nearby rivers such as the PeeDee, Black and Sampit, where Friendfield was located. In 1840, the Georgetown area produced almost half of all the rice grown in the United States. To make this possible, hundreds of slaves were imported each year. In 1740 there were forty thousand slaves in South Carolina—two-thirds of its total population.

Although untold thousands of slaves died in the process, only the blacks could withstand working in the ghastly summer heat, enduring the stench of stagnant water in the rice fields, clouds of malaria-carrying mosquitoes, poisonous snakes, alligators, swamps and the backbreaking task of hewing down cypress, gum and tupelo from the virgin forests and swamps along the river. Hoeing, ditching, planting and sowing were impossible tasks for the white settlers who were not used to such conditions. African slaves were indispensable.

At the height of successful rice growing in the nineteenth century, Friendfield on the Sampit, under the ownership of James Withers's son

In 1818 Francis Withers built this mansion at Friendfield Plantation near the Sampit River. The plantation was originally called Washington before being renamed by Francis Withers in honor of an act of generosity from his brother. *Courtesy of Evelyn Forster Martin.*

Women pounding rice. *Courtesy of the Morgan Collection and the Georgetown County Public Library.*

The Episcopal Parish of Prince George Winyah was founded in 1721. *Postcard collection, courtesy of Ed Carter.*

The old church that burned in 1942. *Courtesy of Frances Cheston Train.*

Francis (1769–1847), encompassed five plantations. Plantations in this sense meant the division of the planted fields, although they were all part of the whole and all of them bordered the Sampit. They were Friendfield, Mount Pleasant (now called Silver Hill), Midway, Harmony (across the Sampit) and Northhampton, which included Bonny Neck and Westfield.

In those days Francis also owned large properties on the Waccamaw Neck and a beachfront property up the line in the present Myrtle Beach area called Withers Swash.

In addition, he owned property on Sandy Island in the Waccamaw, town houses in Charleston and two in Georgetown, a pew in St. Paul's Church in Charleston and one in Prince George Episcopal Church in Georgetown, as well as around five hundred slaves. He was a very rich man for the day or any day. In his will, dated 1847, Francis left numerous bequests to relatives and friends of five thousand dollars each, plus funds for the churches, the Indigo Society and provisions for the care of his slaves. He left money for the upkeep of a meetinghouse he had built for his slaves on Friendfield and enough to pay for a preacher "as long as the people desired it." (This same church—designed in an unusual gothic style—remained until 1940, when it burned along with six of the original cabins on the street.) Although a slave owner like all of his white South Carolina plantation neighbors, Francis was extremely kind and thoughtful. He left his wife "the Friendfield gang of two hundred slaves"

Winyah Indigo Society, founded 1740. The hall was built in 1857. *Postcard collection, courtesy of Ed Carter.*

with the stipulation that the families never be separated, and he made arrangements for an old slave retainer to be housed comfortably with a relative of his in Georgetown for the remainder of her life.

After Francis's first wife, Elizabeth Thomas, died, he married Mrs. Sara Warham, a widow from neighboring Northhampton. She came to live at Friendfield along with her small daughter, Elizabeth Warham. I like to think about this kind man who was devoted to his stepdaughter— eventually leaving her the entire plantation—and who also took in his new wife's mother and her mother-in-law from her first marriage. Perhaps his example created the aura of sweetness and hospitality that has lasted in our house to this day.

Francis built a new Friendfield house in 1818, and according to a newspaper article of the day, it featured decorative wrought-iron railings and elaborate nineteenth-century French scenic wallpaper in the parlor. (Entitled "The Monuments of Paris," the wallpaper was designed in 1814 by Xavier Mader for the French manufacturer Joseph Dufour. An example of the paper is now on display at the Metropolitan Museum of Art in New York City.) A grand circular staircase extended from the ground floor to the attic. There were doorknobs of silver and ceramic, fine oil paintings and an excellent library. Apparently all the notables, including the governor of South Carolina and the mayor of Georgetown, attended the housewarming.

Drawing Room of Friendfield House, Georgetown, S. C.

Paul E. Trouche, publisher, Charleston, S. C. — Germany

The Friendfield Plantation drawing room was elaborately decorated with highly-prized, hand-painted French wallpaper. The elegant mansion built in 1818 by Francis Withers boasted marble fireplaces, silver and Dresden china doorknobs and a spectacular staircase from the cellar to the third-floor attic. *Postcard collection, courtesy of Ed Carter.*

Robert Francis Withers, Francis's cousin, was the original owner of Mount Pleasant (Silver Hill), a lovely old mansion decorated "with style and taste." The cornices, mantelpiece and chair rails from this old house were transferred to the parlor at Friendfield when my father recreated the house in 1930.

In 1822 a tremendous hurricane swept Robert's North Island beach house into the ocean, and his wife and five children were drowned. Robert himself died in 1827 and is buried at Midway in the pinewoods, near those rice fields he knew so well.

There are touching graffiti on the dining room wall at Silver Hill signed in 1838 by Elizabeth Warham and her best friend and cousin, Virginia Wilkinson. Elizabeth was Francis Withers's stepdaughter. She eventually inherited Friendfield and married Dr. Alexis Forster, who ran the plantation after his father-in-law's death in 1848. They wrote: "Farewell to Mt Pleasant...gloom." And it must have been gloomy—the empty mansion fading into the brush and the memory of the poor drowned family haunting the lovely old house.

More graffiti written on the wall of the third-floor bedroom in 1848 reads: "Frances Elizabeth Forster spinster age 17, and Anne Bassile

Friendfield Plantation House before Restoration. *Postcard collection, courtesy of Ed Carter.*

Heriot, spinster age 17." Anne was the daughter of Francis's dear friend Edward Heriot, to whom he left the sum of three thousand dollars, all the wine and liquor from Springfield Plantation and all the cattle from Long Bay. Francis purchased Springfield (part of Brookgreen) in 1800 to help out his friend Benjamin Alston, who named his son Francis Withers Alston—probably in honor of the good deed that enabled him to buy his own property.

After 1848 Mount Pleasant, later Silver Hill, was neither occupied nor altered in any way; that is, until Daniel Thorne, my co-owner, meticulously restored it exactly to its previous splendor. It has been placed on the National Register of Historic Places along with the rest of Friendfield. The old house was so well built that it withstood all of the fierce hurricanes of the eighteenth and nineteenth centuries—even Hugo, whose horrific blast drove a steel tugboat all the way across the Sampit, across the rice fields and right up to the front door. But the old chimneys never lost a brick.

The Forster family had to flee Friendfield in the "dead of night" when the Yankee soldiers were approaching. They returned after the war, but because there was little money, the property fell into sad disrepair. They sold the property to B. Walker Canon; then, in 1919, it was sold to Patrick C. McClary, who rented it to a duck hunting club from Florence. The house burned to the ground in 1926. My father sternly warned us that the house burned because the men got drunk and didn't tend to the log fire. It was a scary lesson for us in a house where every room had an open fireplace.

Friendfield Plantation. *Courtesy of the Georgetown County Museum.*

The arcade at the front door of the modern Friendfield Plantation. *Courtesy of Frances Cheston Train.*

My canoe in the sunken garden. *Courtesy of Frances Cheston Train.*

The monkey puzzle tree landmark as seen from the Sampit River. *Courtesy of Frances Cheston Train.*

My father gradually pieced together numerous small farm holdings that brought the property back to its former antebellum size of thirty-three hundred acres. The land, bordered by White's Creek, Port's Creek and the Sampit River, was a typical Lowcountry mixture of rice fields, marsh, swamp and upland forests of loblolly and longleaf pine, sweet gum, cypress, tupelo, water oak and live oak. It was home to game of all sorts, and was—and is—a hunter's paradise.

In the years before the War Between the States—the Civil War was always called that by Southerners—the rice planters in the Carolina Lowcountry were immensely wealthy and cultured. They often traveled abroad and sent their sons to universities like Harvard. In the eighteenth century the little seaport town of Georgetown, five miles from Friendfield, shipped out more tons of rice—"Carolina Gold," the long grain seed from Madagascar—than any other port in the U.S., and even shipped rice to China.

The 1932 Friendfield House was built under the direction of architect Arthur Meigs of the Philadelphia firm of Mellor and Meigs on the original floor plan, with the exception of one less wing. Pillars two stories

Azaleas below a live oak tree. *Courtesy of the Georgetown County Museum.*

tall support the front porch in classical fashion. A new addition to the original plan is the graceful Italianate arcade that leads up from the sandy driveway in the back and creates a new entrance. The slave street and original cabins have been restored, and the old barnyard and kennels remain just as I remember them from my childhood.

The rooms are big and square with thirteen-foot ceilings and tall windows. A charming floral needlepoint rug brightens up the parlor along with the antique furniture and the ornate gilt pier mirror that reaches from floor to ceiling. The curtains were originally red velvet suitable for one of "Miss Scarlett's" makeover wartime gowns.

My great-great-grandfather Francis Martin Drexel's lovely portrait of a serious little girl hangs over the mantel. The girl is wearing a floor-length red velvet dress, tiny black slippers, a white ruffled cap over her curls and is forever pulling her little toy wooden wagon over the oriental carpet. A fine portrait of Alexander Hamilton, attributed to Robert Fulton, hangs on the far wall.

The children were not allowed to play in the parlor, although we always managed to sneak in and raid the enticing purple tin of Camee

Azaleas with Spanish moss. *Courtesy of the Georgetown County Museum.*

chocolates at their accustomed place on the round mahogany table. If a grown-up should be tempted to look inside, they would find the bottom layer consisted of cleverly concealed "spit-backs"—those icky ones with runny liqueur centers. We thought the room immensely grand, and we tried to behave ourselves when we were invited in.

The library is a cozy room, paneled in cypress, with one semicircular wall with shelves still filled with well-thumbed novels, old and new, wildlife reference books, mysteries and nonfiction tales of adventure. A unique collection of oil paintings by the French painter Raymond Desvarreux of World War I allies in their regimental uniforms hang on the opposite wall over the fireplace. The room is hospitably shabby—a place where hunters plop down in their old clothes to enjoy drinks or tea by the fire, and where dogs are always welcome.

When Pat McClary was a boy in the 1920s he discovered the outlines of a fascinating serpentine water garden, "the sunken garden," that had been carved out from the forest by prodigious slave labor in the eighteenth century. He showed the area to Umberto Innocenti, a famous landscape architect from Florence who had been hired by my father, and they proceeded to direct the restoration of the original gardens. Innocenti designed the decorative brick walls enclosing the camellia garden, paths and fountains.

The water garden was a magical place for me when I was a child, and my children and grandchildren paddle a flat-bottomed boat around the islands just as I once did, pretending to be Native American warriors or pirate captains.

I have never revealed the place where I buried my treasure seventy years ago, or confessed that the brass-bound chest of legend was really a cardboard box containing some pennies, nickels and cookies. However, the crumpled map with its (ketchup) bloodstains and $X$ marking the spot still exists, saved by my mother and father in the desk drawer. My friend Shirley and I signed it, in what we thought of as pirate script: "One-eyed Pete, Captain, and Stinking Bill, Mate."

Friendfield was renowned for its early eighteenth-century experiments with the planting of tea, and Mr. Innocenti identified the original plants that remained and also cleared the ground around a strikingly lovely "pride of India" chinaberry tree. He saved an ancient monkey puzzle tree near the front porch that had served as a landmark beacon for river travelers for many years. Red, white and pink camellias bloom profusely during the winter months, making each glossy, green-leafed bush resemble a decorated Christmas tree. In March, all the glories of spring emerge: azaleas, daffodils, wisteria, jasmine, dogwoods, viburnum, tea olive and gardenias. Later, in May, the powerful sensuous perfume from the huge, waxy-white blooms of *Magnolia grandiflora* drifts in the soft spring air.

On its south side, the house faces out over sweeping lawns toward rice fields and the river. The lawn, planted each fall in Italian ryegrass, is always a startling bright green—even in winter. The giant live oaks in the "big yard," more than two hundred years old, rise in their majesty above the green lawns with plenty of room to spread their massive limbs, draped with graceful curly fronds of silvery gray Spanish moss that trail to the ground.

The shooting ponies love to munch on the moss, but it has no nutritional value. Daddy used to forbid us to bring it into the house because he said the moss harbored ticks and redbugs, but he had no hesitation setting us to work forking it up into piles where it had blown off the trees. He hated to see it scattered over his beautiful lawn. Doing that chore and pulling mustard grass was our main job. Luckily the awful invasion of fire ants with their unsightly mounds had not yet reached South Carolina during his lifetime. Kicking those mounds and hopping out of the way as the tiny red ants pour out to defend their territory is an irresistible pastime, but beware if even one makes it into your shoe or up your pants leg—they do sting like fire!

CHAPTER 3

# My Yankee Life

I was raised on Sandy Run Farm in Oreland, Pennsylvania—a small village near Fort Washington, Montgomery County, Pennsylvania. Sandy Run was originally called Emlen House after its first owners, an eighteenth-century farming family. Solidly built out of Pennsylvania fieldstone, the oldest part of the house was constructed before 1730. During the Revolutionary War, it was General Washington's headquarters for six weeks while his troops were stationed first at Camp Hill, and later at Valley Forge during that fierce December 1777. In the march from Camp Hill to Valley Forge, the cracked and frozen feet of the starving and disheartened soldiers left bloody footprints in the frozen snowdrifts.

I was the youngest of the family. My father, Radcliffe Cheston Jr. (born 1888), married and had two children—George and Sydney. At the end of World War I, his young wife joyfully traveled over to New York from her home in Bryn Mawr, Pennsylvania, to meet his homecoming troop ship. Then tragedy struck their marriage. She fell ill in the hotel where they had their reunion, and within three days she died of the "Spanish flu," leaving the two babies motherless.

The Spanish influenza pandemic of 1918 killed more than 40,000,000 people—a greater mortality than during the four years of the Black Death. At least 675,000 people died in the United States alone.

My mother, Frances Drexel Fell (born 1887), was first married to Antelo Devereux and had two children—a boy and a girl, Antelo and Alix. Tragedy also entered her life when her husband took a bad fall in a hunt meet timber race and suffered incurable amnesia. He was institutionalized and did not recognize her or the children ever again. They were divorced after six sad years.

My mother and father married, and I was their only child together—born in July 1926. We all grew up as one family, and in truth became even

My father and mother after a first-rate turkey hunt. *Courtesy of Frances Cheston Train.*

House where General Washington stayed while in Georgetown, South Carolina. *Postcard collection, courtesy of Ed Carter.*

more than that when my father's daughter Sydney married my mother's son Antelo. It turned out to be a most successful—although unusual—union between a stepsister and stepbrother. Many Philadelphians were kin, but this was the ultimate complexity, and it certainly caused a few tongues to wag. ("Tsk, tsk. Imagine. They were brought up in the same house as brother and sister," et cetera.) Sydney and Antelo remained happily married for over forty years, which made their two sons my double nephews.

An age gap of many years separated me from my brothers and sisters, but our love for each other was close and enduring. I never experienced the sibling rivalries that many of my friends seem to remember, probably because of the big differences in our ages and life experiences. My mother, with her kind and generous nature, never took sides. She took great care to be fair and loving toward her motherless stepchildren, and my father always admired his beautiful stepdaughter and his quiet, gentlemanly stepson. My half brother George told me much later that he always loved my mother as dearly as the image of the mother he had never known.

Except for the semi isolation from school friends who lived too far away for easy visiting, I was cheerful and happy. It didn't dawn on me until much later that my parents were years older than the parents of my classmates. My mother was thirty-nine when I was born; her sister, Aunt Mae Cadwalader, was forty-two when she had my cousin Minnie. This made a difference in their attitude toward child rearing, and probably explained why Minnie and I were left so often with governesses and nurses. After all, our mothers had already raised their much older children, and even had grandchildren by the time I was born.

Over two centuries the farmhouse was gradually enlarged into the big rambling home where I grew up. There were eight family bedrooms with baths in the front part of the house, and the maids' quarters were in the "back hall"—seven small, dreary rooms where some of the "girls" (all Irish immigrants at that time) had to double up. There were two parlormaids, two waitresses, a kitchen maid and a laundress. Each room was sparsely furnished with a bureau, a straight chair and white-painted iron bedsteads with twangy black mesh springs. Jenny, my mother's sweet lady's maid, Annie, the all-important cook, Miss Smith, the English governess—a small, stiffly-corseted woman who always wore pince-nez fastened to her starched bosom by a golden chain—and Margaret, my Scottish Nurse, were deemed superior beings on the domestic totem pole and therefore they had their own modest, but more comfortable, single rooms.

The property consisted of about thirty acres of fields, woods, extensive lawns, flower gardens, orchards and vegetable gardens. There were kennels, stables, garages and my favorite, the berry patches—neat rows of black and red currants, raspberries and gooseberries. The leaves of the plump, pale, green-and-white striped gooseberries were perennial targets for the despised Japanese beetle—a beautiful shiny black and green beetle with prickly black legs that clung to your hand when you picked the luscious tart fruit. Our cook, Annie, was a master of the wonderfully ethereal dessert called "Gooseberry Fool," which I have not tasted since those days many long years ago,

A long cutting garden produced dozens of varieties of flowers for the house, and the green lawns in spring were covered in drifts of daffodils. Beyond a stone bridge that arched over the millrace lay a secret garden with a lily pond, bright with pink and white waterlilies. Their heart shaped leaves made perfect stages for frog concerts. In the pond's center, a bronze statue of the goat-hoofed god Pan piped away, ready to seduce any vulnerable maiden who might chance by. A low stone building, the springhouse, squatted by the edge of the stream, its moss-shingled roof sheltered by towering, piebald-barked sycamores.

The camellia garden at Friendfield. *Courtesy of Frances Cheston Train.*

In the springhouse, clear, icy springs ceaselessly swelled and bubbled up from the limestone bedrock. The farm's extra milk and cream were stored there in silver milk cans, balanced on the flat slabs that projected from the thick stone walls. This was a favorite cooling-off place for me on hot, humid summer afternoons, and I often scooped up handfuls of achingly cold water and laid my sweaty cheek along the sides of the misted, chilled cans.

Our two faithful gardeners—taciturn Pennsylvania Dutchman George Schumm and his little, bouncy assistant, Dominick Pierre, who walked to work from the village about two miles away and trudged home each evening—took care of all this. Two chauffeurs—George Burns, an elderly red-faced Irishman who had been my mother's coachman, and Tommy Dunn, an engaging young Scot who built my treehouse and taught me all sorts of useful carpentry—were in charge of the garage. I spent many hours with them, probably bothering them to death, but they were unfailingly kind and cheerful—as was all the jolly, mothering Irish help. My days as the youngest child were never lonely and almost always interesting. It was an upstairs/downstairs life. The downstairs part occupied most of my non-school time, with the exception of the never-to-be-missed radio programs between 5:00 and 7:00 p.m. —*Dick Tracy, Little Orphan Annie, Jack Armstrong* and the rest of the gang.

My maternal grandparents, Alexander and Sarah Drexel Van Rensselaer, lived about a mile from us on the crest of Camp Hill in an ugly stone castle–like mansion, turreted and crenellated and typical of a certain type of nineteenth-century Philadelphia architecture. They were an unpretentious couple, who liked nothing more than having their large extended family over for informal tea parties and picnics, saving their fancier entertaining for the big town house at 18th and Walnut Streets on the corner of Rittenhouse Square in Philadelphia.

Sarah's father, my great-grandfather Anthony J. Drexel (1826–1893), was a successful banker in the firm Drexel & Co., founded by his father, Francis. He amassed a large fortune, and his philanthropy was widespread. He took on a young New Yorker, J.P. Morgan, and the firm became Drexel, Morgan & Co. with branches in Paris, New York and London. Mr. Drexel hated publicity of any kind and was remembered as a man "of singular modesty," who "feared and shamed praise more than blame." Morgan went on to found his own firm stating, "Tony Drexel will never get anywhere, he's too damn nice."

Anthony Drexel founded the Drexel University of Technology in Philadelphia on the innovative premise that the children of the working classes should be able to study the new sciences of the day and relate their practical application to business, industry or the home, following the student's own career objectives. To implement this, the student was required to spend more than one third of his college life working for a salary, which he used to pay tuition.

The Drexels, of Austrian descent, were Catholic and extremely religious. Their niece, Katherine (1858–1955), became a nun who devoted her whole life and twenty-million-dollar inheritance to found mission schools throughout the West and South for the benefit of "Indians" (Native Americans) and "Negroes" (African Americans). Katherine became a respected friend to Chief Red Cloud of the Sioux nation. This tiny, fierce lady once famously faced down angry members of the Ku Klux Klan on the steps of her church in New Orleans when they tried to intimidate her because of her advanced ideas on racial equality. It is said that the Klan's headquarters were struck by lightning that same week. She made it a strict rule in her churches and schools that there be no segregated seating, and she founded Xavier University in New Orleans—the first Negro University in the U.S.—all of this thirty years before the start of the civil rights movement. Pope John Paul II canonized her Saint Katherine in the year 2000.

The *May* and crew. *Top row:* The woman in the white dress is Sarah Drexel Fell Van Rensselear; the little boy is John Fell. Standing to her right is Alexander Van Rensselear. The girl in the white dress in the front is Frances Drexel Fell. The lady in the hat is Mae Drexel Fell. *Courtesy of Frances Cheston Train.*

The Van Rensselaers owned the *May*, a beautiful steel, schooner-rigged steam yacht. The *May* was built in 1891, weighing 766 tons and measuring 240 feet over all, with a 27-foot beam and 14.5-foot draft. She had a crew of 40, counting the officers, chefs, engineers, stokers and sailors. The yacht's interior was as luxurious as a palace, with working fireplaces, gas-fitted lights, paneled rooms, a library full of books, a formal dining room with silver candelabra and silk brocade curtains and bedspreads in the staterooms.

With all these luxurious trappings, the family was extremely unassuming and polite, always considerate of the feelings of their employees and democratic and humorous in their dealings. Consequently, they were much loved and respected, and the people who worked for them stayed on forever—in many cases until they died "in service." It was very much a Quaker attitude that permeated Philadelphia society at that time.

They cruised everywhere on the *May*. Up and down the coastal U.S., across the Atlantic to England, France and even India, and they took

The schooner *City of Georgetown. Postcard collection, courtesy of Ed Carter.*

along their children and a dog or two on their trips. During their longer voyages they left the children in Paris or London to make up some school time, but once when they went to Egypt, my mother was allowed to stay on board. In a bazaar in Cairo, she secretly purchased a bandaged object from a street peddler, who assured her it was the "mummified hand of Queen Nefertiti." She was thrilled to be in possession of such a valuable and unique souvenir, and she successfully hid it in her bureau on the yacht until a terrible smell was traced to her stateroom. After the bandage was unwrapped, the hand of the queen was discovered to be the decomposing paw of a dog.

My father's family was composed of respected, professional people. Grandfather Cheston was a much beloved country doctor who treated every kind of ailment and counseled his patients long before anyone started going to shrinks. He delivered babies, and in fact even brought me into the world, much to the embarrassment of my mother who didn't like the idea of her own father-in-law being her obstetrician—tea in the parlor one day, into the stirrups the next. Daddy always visited his Grandfather James on the Western Shore of Maryland for vacations, and it was there in the marshes and farms where he discovered his lifelong love of wildlife and nature—gifts that he passed on to me.

Kids' lives were not highly organized in those days. Parents rarely, if ever, visited their schools, hardly knew the names of the teachers and never turned out for sports events. No one had to drive us to ballet or soccer practice. Music teachers came to the house (dreaded scales!), the tennis instructor came to my aunt's court next door and for everything else we made up our own fun. Largely for this reason, I found vacations at the plantation fascinating. There was always an adventure or something out of the ordinary going on.

My siblings and I were brought up under the stern motto of "never explain, never complain." I learned to turn the serious into a joke and to conceal any troubles. If you fell off your bike and skinned your knee, you received stinging iodine and very little comfort—not like today when there is a pill for every ailment and a psychiatrist for anxiety or depression. I was expected to behave, to be obedient and polite, to see the other point of view and, above all, to never hurt anyone's feelings or question parental authority.

This was the characteristic attitude that permeated Philadelphia society at the time. By today's standards, readers may wonder why many of my generation were so complacent—so accepting and "un-curious"—but that's exactly the way it was for those of us brought up in our particular milieu. During my teen and preteen years, because of World War II, travel abroad was out of the question and even travel in the states was greatly curtailed. We were naïve and insular and overprotected.

In spite of my parents' wealth, our habits were frugal by today's standards. Very few things were ever thrown away. Men's collars were turned, sheets and socks darned, hems let down and raised and lights snapped off as soon as one left the room. I had an unrealistically small allowance—twenty-five cents a week—and absolutely no knowledge about money. All practical needs were provided for, but most requests for extras were refused. In those days, household help often spent their entire working lives in the service of one family—forty or fifty years sometimes—and then counted on their employers to see them through their old age. There were no Social Security or government welfare programs at that time, and household employees were considered part of the family.

My only personal contact with the trials of the Great Depression was the lunches my family provided twice a week for groups of shabby men who made their way across the fields from their shanty towns—"hobo jungles"—along the Reading Railroad tracks a few miles away. We called these men "tramps," although not to their face. They wore mismatched dark suits and leather town shoes, and were invariably polite and grateful for the heaping plates of Irish stew the cook served up to them on our back porch. I often sat out there with them, listening to their jokes and especially their harmonica playing, a talent one of them unsuccessfully tried to teach me. There was never a hint that they were potential thieves, drunkards or unfit companions for a child, and everyone in our household thought them to be decent men who were simply down and out in that time of widespread unemployment.

I didn't know what my father did at work—a place he disappeared to everyday on the train—except that he had the enviable position of being the president of the Philadelphia Zoo. He saw to it that we had a procession of exotic pets—a kinkajou, alligators, an ocelot, parrots, canaries, raccoons, dogs of all sorts and Mike, my rhesus monkey. Mike forever disgraced himself by burying his little black hands in a ripe camembert cheese, sniffing and grimacing disdainfully, then flicking the smelly, creamy goo all over my fastidious Uncle Gouvie Cadwalader's immaculate linen suit and silk tie.

Daddy also thought that a pair of white rats would be just the thing to amuse me while I was recovering in a darkened room from the measles. I used to let them out to run over my bed, and once I picked one up by the tail because my big brother George—an awful tease—told me that when you picked a guinea pig up by the tail its eyes would fall out. This never happened when I swung poor Ratty to and fro. Of course, I didn't realize that guinea pigs had no tails! Later, as a reward for my long incarceration, I was given a spotted pony called, naturally, Measles.

Personal vanity was frowned upon in my semi-Victorian Philadelphia Quaker-style upbringing. My family had a beautiful collection of Japanese Netsuke ornaments made of carved ivory. These were kept in a glass-fronted cabinet on the second-floor landing of our big front staircase. Once, when I was about twelve years old, I paused on the stairs to look into the cabinet and I could see my reflection in the case's mirrored backing.

In the mirror, I saw my father coming up soundlessly behind me. "Who do you think you're looking at?" his reflection challenged.

"No one," I whispered, and fled upstairs to my third-floor bedroom, ashamed of—what? I didn't fully understand. Ever since, I have been

Girls on a joggling board. *Courtesy of Dr. H.M. Huck's family collection and the Georgetown County Museum.*

reluctant to spend much time in front of a mirror. It might be better if I did, but then I have always been a tomboy.

At home in Whitemarsh, Pennsylvania, I practically lived in a treehouse, beautifully crafted by my best pal Tommy Dunn, the chauffeur, with my "help." It was set up in an old gnarled apple tree like a real little house, with a shingle roof and windows that opened. It had a trapdoor with a secret latch, and a rope ladder that you could pull up to keep out snoopy grown-ups, as well as those unlucky children who weren't allowed in our Cousins' Club. I spent long hours up there, daydreaming that I was in the topmost branches of an African rainforest. (Years later, after I was married, I visited my old apple tree and discovered to my chagrin that those topmost branches were only about fifteen feet off the ground.)

I always loved climbing trees, and my hero in those days was Tarzan. I read every book about his jungle adventures that I could lay my hands on, many of them reprinted in those wonderful kid-size Big Little Books. I would fearlessly imitate him, swinging down from my treehouse on a rope, leaping onto the back of my stuffed donkey (the lion of course) and stabbing him with a wooden dagger until his sawdust ran out.

Once, when I was about eight years old, my mother called me downstairs from my third-floor nursery to introduce me to some British relatives, the Countess of Winchselsea (Cousin Margaretta Drexel) and her son Christopher Finch-Hatten (cousin of Denys, the big game hunter and lover of *Out of Africa* writer Isak Dinesen.)

I had just "fashioned" (I often thought in Edgar Rice Burrough's language) a loincloth by pinning two washcloths together over my cotton underpants, and I swung down the three flights of stairs, Tarzan style, twirled around the newel posts, beat my little flat chest, gave the yodeling cry of the bull ape and landed in my best ape crouch in the middle of the tea party. I guess my mother was mortified, but the British guests were too polite to question what sort of strange little daughter the family kept in the attic.

My entire life has been reflected in the looking glass of my cozy, happy country childhood. Perhaps it left me lacking competitiveness, avoiding confrontation and with few defenses against adversity, but it gave me valuable lessons and insights about understanding, trust and forgiveness—these traits have served me well over the years.

The fact that my brothers and sisters were so much older made me accustomed to being sort of an only child. I was never lonely and always stayed out of doors in the natural world as much as possible—I was conditioned by my jolly Scottish nurse, as well as my outdoor-loving mother and father, to play outside no matter what the weather. Being a voracious reader, I was happy living in a world of imagination even when I was without playmates my own age. The time spent in a kid's paradise like the Carolina Lowcountry was a living dream, and it has been woven into the fabric of my life ever since.

CHAPTER 4

# Plantation Life

E ver since my father bought the plantation in 1930 it has belonged to
our family, and now Daniel Thorne is the principal owner together
with family shareholders. It is rare nowadays in America for a property to
pass down through the generations, and it is especially poignant to watch
children and grandchildren respond to the timeless beauty and charm of
this old rice plantation, just as I did seventy-seven years ago.

When my father started the restoration project, the property surrounding
the "Big House" was overgrown by thick brush, and visitors had to push
their way up through the tangles of vines and brambles from the landing
at White's Creek to the original house site. Only the avenue of ancient live
oaks, the chimneys and part of the foundations remained standing. My
father's guide was Pat McClary, son of the last owner, who soon became
our first manager. Daddy called Pat from his home in Philadelphia to
suggest that he start off his job on a trial basis, "because you might not
suit me after we get going."

Pat, a proud Southerner, replied, "I agree to that, Mr. Cheston,
because you are a Yankee and you might not suit *me.*" The "trial," not
without some hot arguments, lasted forty-two years.

The sentimental thrill of arriving at Friendfield is the same today as it
was when I was little. I felt just like Dorothy after the tornado deposited her
in the Technicolor dream world of Oz when I left the drab, gray Northern
winter and then drove under the glossy-leaved avenue of magnolias,
through the old brick gates to the "Big House," set in its lawns of brilliant
green Italian ryegrass. The house staff in their colorful madras uniforms
gathered on the steps to greet the family. "Ooh, Miss Frances, how BIG
you've grown." They smiled and hugged me, and I was home again—a
little Yankee girl adopted into the warm, colorful world of the South.

Friendfield House in the 1930s. *Courtesy of Frances Cheston Train.*

Pat McClary, the superintendent at Friendfield for forty-two years. *Courtesy of Frances Cheston Train.*

Northerners who owned hunt plantations in Georgetown County often arrived in the area by train. During the Depression, a spur to Georgetown was discontinued and passengers finished the journey by automobile. In a 1937 photo, Belle Baruch and Varvara Hasselbalch disembark at Kingstree to be driven to Hobcaw Barony. *Courtesy of the Belle W. Baruch Foundation.*

My children take just as much delight in the old house as I do, and we have never stopped appreciating the delicious Southern cooking and baking—cornbread, hot biscuits (with butter balls and honey), venison, quail, wild turkey, cooter soup (made from the local yellow-bellied marsh turtle), sweet yams, cheese grits, crabmeat, shrimp, pecan pie and prune soufflé. Now as I write this in 2007 my grandchildren still respect the old traditions, and even in these days of casual dress they enjoy changing for dinner in the formal dining room—such a difference from their pick-up meals at home. The beautifully set mahogany table under its crystal chandelier, the candlelight, the centerpiece of camellias and the hot, sparking pinewood fire giving off its resin smell creates an evocative memory for every age.

Up until the late 1950s the plantation workers and tenant farmers lived in small, whitewashed cabins scattered throughout the property. We knew all of the families, cared about them and visited them often. They raised many children, tended small gardens and kept a few pigs, chickens and a plowing mule. We thought they were happy and carefree, and they greeted

Slave cabins on the street near Friendfield Plantation. *Courtesy of Frances Cheston Train.*

us with unfailing courtesy and frequent smiles. Some cabins were scattered throughout the property, and eight of the old slave quarters where many families lived during the 1930s and '40s still exist on each side of the "street"—a white sand road leading out back from the "Big House" to the barnyard. The houses were set up two feet off the ground on brick pillars, away from the rising damp or visiting snakes. Some of the bricks are more than two hundred years old and are greatly prized today by people wanting to restore old buildings. Electricity and running water were not installed until the 1940s.

I used to go there almost every day to play marbles and skip rope with the children. I didn't go inside the cabins for some reason—perhaps it wasn't allowed—but I remember peeking into the dark rooms whose walls were covered with newspapers for insulation. Typically there were three rooms: two small bedrooms and one bigger room for eating, sitting and cooking over an open hearth. Sometimes there was a loft that could be reached by a homemade ladder, and some cabins were double, lived in by two families. The light came from kerosene lanterns, but everyone turned in as soon as it grew dark.

There was an outhouse about twenty yards in the back, and an outdoor hand pump at the well. I loved to prime the pump with water from the tin

Arcadia, where General LaFayette spent his first night in America. Georgetown, South Carolina. *Postcard collection, courtesy of Ed Carter.*

Arcadia Plantation. *Courtesy of the Georgetown County Museum.*

cup always left full nearby. The handle made a tremendous squeaking and clanking noise, and then came the squelch of suction and the satisfying gush of water. The washing was done in the yard in a big cast-iron, three-legged pot and a hot pinewood fire heated the water.

Small gardens were planted with early collard greens in the winter months. In the spring and summer, larger communal gardens grew yams, watermelons, peas and beans. The men were keen hunters of deer, possum, squirrel, raccoon and rabbit, and there were always catfish, flounder, bream, mullet, turtles, blue crabs and shrimp to be caught or trapped in the rice field ponds and ditches. I'm sure more than a few ducks were bagged when the boss was up North.

Pat told me a story about a man over on George Vanderbilt's Arcadia Plantation who killed his wife's lover. He was convicted of murder and sentenced to the chain gang for life. At the same time, another man from Arcadia was convicted of poaching wood ducks and was sentenced to four months in jail.

But the murderer happened to be Mr. Vanderbilt's cook—a good one—and Mr. Vanderbilt wanted him back. So Mr. V. had a few words with the sheriff and had the murderer sprung after a week. The poacher complained from his cell: "What kind of a State we live in, when de law turn a man loose for murder, and I serve four months in de jail house fo' getting' me a few ducks?"

The families in the cabins always showed us deferential kindness and humor but their inner lives and thoughts were hidden from us. It was years before I understood the survival mechanisms of Southern "coloreds"—always agree and give the answer that white folks expect and come up with an ingenious excuse.

"Yassuh Boss, I done wash de dishes keerful lak you always done 'splain me, but dat plate seem lak it tuk wings an fly from me han' by he ownself lak a quail." Just about everyone who worked for us in those days spoke Gullah and we Northerners became fairly adept at understanding, but not speaking, the dialect.

In the house, Maggie and Liza were the chambermaid and waitress. During duck hunting seasons, in addition to their daily duties, they were expected to rise at five and light the pinewood fires in the icy bedrooms for those hunters going out early to the blinds.

Drayton, the butler, took justifiable pride in his duties and ruled over the cook, Miss Florence, and the rest of the household with total authority. The women in the house almost always deferred to the men.

David Drayton, the butler before Peter Small *Courtesy of Frances Cheston Train.*

Drayton carved the meat, filleted the shad, cut up the venison, passed the drinks and waited on the table.

I watched when he butchered a cooter (yellow-bellied marsh turtle) or a snapping turtle for the dinner table. He looped a rope around a sturdy stick then teased the turtle until it made a lightning-fast snapping bite to grab and hold on with its sharp, beak-like jaws. He demonstrated how to pull the stick away slowly so that the poor turtle extended its neck, and then he chopped off its head with one quick blow of the axe. I looked on, appalled, while the turtle crawled about, headless and bleeding. The warning went that if a snapper ever latched on to you, he wouldn't let go until there was a thunderstorm. Afterwards, I was supposed to enjoy the soup, even when I spotted its little tail and claws floating about in the broth with the carrots and meat.

My father tried, without success, to make me eat live oyster crabs—tiny, crisp critters that ran about on top of a raw oyster served on the half shell. I tried it once. When I reluctantly gulped down the slippery oyster, the little crab escaped and scurried across my tongue until I could catch it between my teeth with a crunch! Never again, I vowed, though fried oyster crabs and whitebait were a prime delicacy for the grown-ups.

Something else that no kid could stomach was a whole roast duck, served on huge, individual blue willow-patterned dinner plates. The knives used at the table were razor-sharp, wooden-handled steak knives—suitable for surgery. The mallards were enormous, the teal more dainty, but the way of cooking was early caveman. First of all, the ducks were hung until gamey, and when you slit into the plump breast of your bird the blood spurted out in a jet that would have pleased Count Dracula himself. Often a slice would reveal a little round lead shot, surrounded by its own gooey blood clot. The quail were just as daunting. To tenderize them, they were hung in the cooler for days, which made them taste and smell "high." Eating them properly—that is, gnawing the carcass—required liberal hand washing in fingerbowls. Naturally, the cook thought cooking meat rare was a barbarous Yankee custom, but they obliged just the same.

Once, I remember, at a picnic in the woods, Pat surreptitiously ordered Peter (our butler who succeeded Drayton) to put his quail back on the fire for some more cooking. "The Boss must tink I be some kin' Blue Darter Hawk for to eat my quail raw." Southerners like their meat well done, or fried or boiled.

Our cooks, first Florence and then Annie Small, were enormously talented and soon adapted to the peculiar tastes of the Boss and his family. The indigenous cooking—like crispy crab cakes, fried chicken and shrimp gumbo—was delicious. Perfectly cooked rice was a ubiquitous companion.

Boats along the riverfront in Georgetown. *Courtesy of Dr. H.M. Huck's family collection and the Georgetown County Museum.*

They were often asked to duplicate unfamiliar and complex recipes, which had to be read to them, but they soon learned skills comparable or superior to their Northern counterparts. Here is an extraordinarily calorific and time-consuming recipe for cooking the saltwater terrapins that used to be trapped along with the cooters in our rice field marsh. I found it just a few years ago in a jumble of penciled recipes stuffed in a kitchen drawer.

*Terrapin for Four People*

*Scald and remove all outside shell. Boil young terrapin for at least 1½ hours. After boiling, break apart and remove liver carefully so as not to break gall. Cut meat into medium size pieces. Remove large bones. Remove eggs and reserve. Use a slow fire, and never let the cream sauce boil, nor the sauce and terrapin meat when mixing. Do not stir terrapin meat and cream sauce when mixing—shake the saucepan.*

*Cream sauce:*
*1 quart pure cream*
*½ pound butter*
*Flour to make a roux. Mix in a little terrapin stock.*
*Cook the butter and flour to make a paste and stir in cream gradually.*

Oysterman in front of oyster beds. *Courtesy of the Georgetown County Museum.*

Fishing boats. *Postcard collection, courtesy of Ed Carter.*

*Terrapin butter:*
*3 hard-boiled egg yokes*
*2 tablespoons corn starch*
*¼ cup butter*
*Mix thoroughly and mash egg yokes with spoon. Mix with cream sauce. Add salt, nutmeg and cayenne pepper. Cook sauce and terrapin meat together slowly by shaking the pan, not stirring, and add sherry or Madeira to taste. Arrange terrapin eggs around sides of serving platter. Ladle over ½ of a baked potato, which has been served on the plate first.*

I also found a delicious recipe for boula soup that requires a pint of green turtle pieces mixed with a purée of green peas, stock from "an old hen" and "plenty" of sherry. Green turtles were not endangered then. Another complicated recipe—one for gumbo file—closed with the admonition *requiescat in pace.* There was plenty of Scotch whiskey, brandy and cocktail mixings available for the guests (after Prohibition).

*Philadelphia Fish House Punch*

*For 1½ gallons*
*1½ cups sugar*

Rene Cathou using a table saw. *Photo by Jerry Caines. Courtesy of the Georgetown County Museum.*

*1 quart fresh lemon juice*
*2 quarts 100-proof Jamaican rum*
*2 quarts cold water*
*4 ounces peach brandy*
*1 quart cognac*
*1 block of ice*
*1 cup sliced fresh peaches (That will do the business!)*

There was a so-called wine cellar in a backroom behind the coal furnace and I remember jars of corn liquor stored on a shelf. They bought them from a farmer/bootlegger up by Hell Hole Swamp in Williamsburg County, where we owned property for our Black River quail shoot. They called it "stump juice" or "white lightning." One shot was plenty to light your fire internally or perhaps to ignite a blaze in the fireplace. *WHOOSH!*

The twenty-three-mile expedition to McClellanville to buy oysters was a treat I always looked forward to. There was a fish and shrimp dock right on the edge of the creek that led out to Bulls Bay, and the shrimp boats were moored close alongside the rickety wharfs. They were business-like

Rene Cathou's fishing boats. *Courtesy of Joey Cathou and the Georgetown County Museum.*

boats with feminine names and huge brown nets drooping from the masts. Inside a big warehouse with a cement floor were barrels and barrels of iced, fresh oysters. Men were hosing down the oysters to clean them, so the floor was always wet and smelled briny and fishy. Great piles of white oyster shells were stacked out back, and greedy seagulls skimmed down and around, seeking scraps.

The oystermen used heavy fifteen-foot-long wooden poles fitted with iron rakes to tong the oysters from their muddy reefs. It was backbreaking labor, standing for hours balanced on their little wooden skiffs. No matter what the hour by the clock, they had to fish the tide. I think Daddy paid the fisherman about six dollars for a bushel of "selects"; that is, single oysters, not clusters, which were cheaper but not as desirable.

Under a corrugated, tin-roofed, open-sided shed, a long row of women sat on wooden benches, beheading shrimp and throwing the little translucent bodies into enamel pans. They gossiped and laughed and sang while they worked long hours, joining each other in their church songs. One would sing the verse in a lilting, strong soprano, and the others would copy in response. They wore white uniforms, and their brown arms were sleek and muscular. Singing made their task seem easier.

Cathou's Fish House. *Photo by Jerry Caines. Courtesy of the Georgetown County Museum.*

We bought all our fish, except the oysters, from a famous Georgetown character, Mr. Rainy "Rene" Cathou. His place of business was—and still remains—a weather-beaten shack on the edge of the Front Street shrimp docks on the Sampit. I used to love going there with Peter to pick up a shad for the household. Mr. Cathou, red-faced and always wearing a small, straw porkpie fedora, would be sitting there on a rickety kitchen chair by the iron woodstove, entertaining friends and co-workers with pithy stories, gossip and caustic commentary delivered in his blurry Southern accent.

He would listen to our request and summon a worker to fetch a fresh silver shad from a big bucket out on the dock. A scarred, blackish, wooden worktable sat under the window, gleaming with the residue of years and years of fish scales. The helper skillfully scraped our fish, gutted it, extracted the roe and wrapped it in the *Georgetown Times*. ("Only thing it's good for!" said Rene.)

The shad fishermen often caught sturgeon in their nets. These anadromous, prehistoric-looking fish traveled from the Atlantic Ocean

C.L. Ford Residence. Georgetown, South Carolina. *Postcard collection, courtesy of Ed Carter.*

into Winyah Bay on their way upriver to spawn. At the present, the taking of sturgeon is strictly prohibited, but back then in the 1940s it was overlooked as an accidental result of entanglement in the shad nets.

We were longtime customers of Mr. Cathou's fish market, and nothing was more prized and appreciated by our incredulous guests than his half-pound jars of fresh caviar. I once stood on the wharf watching with amazement as a couple of brawny workers sliced open that strange-looking fish and dumped the roe into a galvanized washtub. It took both men to lug it into the fish shack where the preparation took place. This was a simple procedure that involved placing the caviar in a big strainer, rinsing and shaking it under the old iron tap, salting it slightly, removing the membranes, spooning it into the jars and sealing it. I think the cost was five dollars per half-pound jar.

Drayton was the only one who knew how to surgically remove the daunting network of tiny, forked shad bones. Peter, his successor, used needle-nosed pliers to attempt to bone the shad, but too many bones were always left, which inhibited the enjoyment of that delectable fish—the hungrier I was, the more bones I found in each mouthful. The Southern cooking method was to bake the shad for hours until the bones dissolved, but we Northerners preferred them broiled.

A favorite spring pastime was an expedition to go crabbing in the creek behind Pawley's Island where the McClary family had a "shack," as people traditionally called their beach cottages on the island. "Shabby chic" is the Island motto to this day.

Front Street. Georgetown, South Carolina. *Postcard collection, courtesy of Ed Carter.*

First we would stop at Mr. C.L. Ford's store on Front Street—a marvelous emporium that sold everything necessary for the survival and happiness of the citizens of Georgetown. The store was right on the river where boats could pull up to their dock and deliver or pick up goods. An article from the *Georgetown Times*, dated 1994, remembered that "you could purchase anything from canned rattlesnake to caviar." One side contained hardware, a complete ship's chandlery and all sorts of fishing gear, and the other was the grocery. Mr. Ford stocked the best cuts of beef, pork and fresh chickens, as well as rice, beans and wine. He catered to the rich plantation owners as well as the poorer citizens.

Mr. Archer Huntington, owner of "Brookgreen," once ordered a donkey and a Ford automobile and charged it to his grocery account. He went to the store shortly before the market crash in 1929 and gave Mr. Ford a check for ten thousand dollars so he could continue to carry his customers' charge accounts. The store continued on pleasing its many customers until 1961.

I remember it well. When we went to pick up some chicken parts to bait the crab lines, we'd ask the butcher who worked at the back of the store to chop us up some pieces. *WHACK!* went the razor sharp cleaver on the old concave chopping block. Once the pieces were wrapped up in pinkish butcher paper, he would scrape the leftovers into a hole in the far end of

A family fishing trip. *Courtesy of Dr. H.M. Huck's family collection and the Georgetown County Museum.*

the table and they would drop with a splash right into the river below the store—an easy, quick method for garbage disposal in those days.

Pat's dock was reached by means of a rickety wooden walkway out into the creek. It had benches, and a pavilion-like roof that gave shade from the summer's heat. The kids and I would lie on our stomachs on the well-worn boards of the dock, warmed by the welcome spring sunshine, tie a chicken leg or back on the line, weight it and wait impatiently for the first characteristic crabby nibble. Slowly, hand over hand, you pulled up the string and your designated netter would try to scoop them up before they let go and disappeared into the muddy depths. There were many recriminations and accusations when the netter proved too slow or inept, but in the end we used to bring home buckets of snapping, bubbling crabs after these wonderful afternoons. Once on the way home, one of the containers tipped over in the trunk of the car and all the crabs made their way into the compartment behind the back seat. Drayton had to pull the whole seat out to make sure none had taken up residence inside the car before my father found out the hard way a few days later.

I had made it a rule that no fish or crab could be eaten until my children had cleaned and scaled it, or picked out the meat themselves. This curtailed any excessive catch and subsequent waste. We'd all sit around the kitchen table, laughing and listening to gospel singing on the radio and getting a lot of good-natured help and advice from Annie or

Four workers. *Courtesy of Dr. H.M. Huck's family collection and the Georgetown County Museum.*

Women workers. *Courtesy of Dr. H.M. Huck's family collection and the Georgetown County Museum.*

one of the staff. Some child once asked how you could tell a boy crab from a girl crab and was told that the lines on the white underside of the crabs were different. "Boys" had a pendulous "necktie" design and "girls" a "purse." This is true, but we figured out much later the proper anatomical male or female descriptions of necktie and purse. Those fresh blue claw crabs were delicious, and the whole household looked forward to our Pawley's Island outings.

Drayton always ate his meals standing up, leaning against the pantry counter with one elbow as he forked the food into his mouth. He told me: "I bin a steward in the United States Navy, and I got a habit of eatin' dat way." (As the only man on the indoor staff, I think he wanted to avoid eating in the kitchen with the household of women.) He was an upstanding, dignified man, and the money he saved from his job helped educate his son, who became principal of the local school and the first black resident of Georgetown to earn a master's degree. We were always very proud of him.

Later on, Liza's only daughter got her doctorate in education and became principal of a special education school in Harlem. She traveled to conferences all over Europe. When Liza retired, she bought her "maum" a tidy brick house on Queen Street in Georgetown, and we often visited her there. Liza was a wise and exceptional lady.

Store and old slave cabins at Hobcaw's Friendfield Village. *Courtesy of the Georgetown County Museum.*

After Reconstruction, the streets of Georgetown were not segregated, and the houses of blacks and whites were and are situated in the same block. Georgetown boasted the first black to serve in the U.S. House of Representatives, Joseph Rainey (the second black to serve in Congress, following Hiram Revels), and civility between the races is still a hallmark of our town.

In those days, and even in the present-day, older women—both black and white—were always called by the title "Miss" before their first name. I am still "Miss Frances" at the age of eighty, and our cook, age seventy-eight, is "Miss Pauline." The white men were always called "Capt'n" or "Mister" followed by their first name. My older brother once told me wistfully, "When I go back North, I always miss being called 'Capt'n George.'"

When I was growing up, the house servants wore ankle-length, full-skirted, madras plaid dresses with matching turbans and starched white aprons. Today that domestic uniform would be considered unacceptable. They were the kindest, most loving people, and their

Families at Friendfield. *Courtesy of Frances Cheston Train.*

special blend of sympathetic friendship and religious faith remains a constant, comforting and inspiring memory.

The cabins for the outdoor workers were on the street "back of the Big House." There were no porches, and the women and old folks sat on their front steps, smoking their white clay pipes, just resting and sunning and gossiping, watching the "chilluns" at play. I loved talking to Reverend Blackwell—a sweet and wise old gentleman—and I remember visiting with him when he was sitting on his step, holding his grandbaby. An ancient Gullah woman called Ma'am Pleasant happened to walk by. She was noted for her unpleasant disposition, and she complained to me: "Lookit at dat wuthless ol' man. He love he grand too much, so he cain't stan' fer a fly to light on her. Too bad he ain't pay de same attention to us'uns needin' de wood split and chores handle."

When her husband, Jim, a lovely quiet soul, was dying, she was heard to say, "Why that old fool take so long to die anyway? I wish de Lawd would come down and tak him up right now so we don't haf to bin waitin' around dis away." She was one mean old woman.

I remember "Rev" walking along at the edge of the swamp in his faded denim bib overalls, trying to herd a scraggly line of black and white spotted piglets that were racing to the corn trough. He kept on chastising them with a long stick, as though they were his disobedient children: "Hey, pig what you doin'? Stop that foolin'. Git along this way or I'm gonna whup yo' rear end! Yo' sho' goin' make me a fine barbeque, if yo' don't mind me!"

James Graham's and Tom Joyner's children. *Courtesy of Frances Cheston Train.*

The cabin windows had no screens. At nightfall the shutters were closed to keep out the "ha'nts" (ghosts), especially the dreaded plat-eye. The plat-eye possessed a supernatural ability to imitate the familiar voice of a family member. At nighttime, it was said to lure many a person out of bed, enticing the victim to a watery death in the swamp. There really were some incidents of drowning in the swamp, but the plat-eye that killed these victims was actually hallucination and delusion brought about by the high fever of malaria or yellow fever, the scourges of earlier plantation living.

Wesley Bright, his wife Maybell and their kids were another of our favorite families. Their eldest daughter was the beautiful and errant Ruth, who kept running away with different men. Another daughter, Jessie May, the boys Curtis and Wesley Jr. and the triplets Alvin, Alton and Annette, were packed together in their small cabin at the barnyard. The Bright household wasn't the most crowded. Tom Joyner, the dog man and huntsman, and his jolly wife Dolly had ten "head" of children under their roof—it seemed as if each year there was another adorable baby. Tom joked that he wasn't exactly sure how many there were, and when my own daughter Frances was about seven or eight, Dolly told her that she "plumb done run out of names." She asked Frances to suggest a name for their youngest baby. Frances said without hesitation, "Call her Pollyanna."

In a circa 1905 photo, Friendfield Plantation on the Waccamaw River, which is part of Hobcaw, still had nearly fifty residents in its former slave village. The plantation was one of eleven contiguous tracts that Bernard Baruch purchased between 1905 and 1907, reassembling the colonial Hobcaw Barony. Note there are twelve extant structures as well as a church used by freed slaves and their descendants. Most Northerners who purchased Georgetown County plantations hired tenants and provided housing, firewood and transportation to town. *Courtesy of the Belle W. Baruch Foundation.*

"Lawd hab mussy, dat's a sweet name," Dolly beamed, and so the baby was christened.

That name turned out to be lucky. About thirty years later, Pollyanna drove up to the "Big House" in a fancy black sedan, wearing a beautiful mink coat. She was showing her husband the plantation and the rickety little cabin where she had been brought up. I was delighted to meet her again, and to learn that she held a surgical nursing degree from Stanford University. She and her husband lived in San Francisco where he was a successful medical malpractice lawyer.

Many children were brought up in those tiny cabins. The school bus showed up every day for the McClary children—Clebe, Patty and Virginia—but if the black kids wanted to go to school they had to walk the five miles into Georgetown to the Howard School. Some were successful later like Pollyanna, but many weren't. Were they really happy? Did they complain? I never knew, but I did learn that Wesley drank too much.

Pat told me that when he bailed Wesley out of jail for the umpteenth time, he told him: "Wesley! Good Lawd, man, why you keep on doin' that way when y'all know how much aggravation it causes?"

Interior of the Episcopal Parish of Prince George Winyah, built in 1736. *Postcard collection, courtesy of Ed Carter.*

Wesley grinned his delightful grin, and answered, "Capt'n Pat, you just ain't never been a nigger on Saturday night." In those days, African Americans referred to themselves by that word, and it was often part of a colloquial dialogue on such popular radio programs as *Amos and Andy*. Our staff listened to every episode on their little staticky kitchen radio. You could hear them laughing uproariously and commenting on the comical doings of Kingfish, Sapphire and company all the way into the front of the house.

Wesley lived to a ripe old age in spite of his carousing. I went to his funeral service and walked up to the altar to say goodbye to him and thank him for all our good times together when I was a child, and for the friendship shared by his many children and mine over the years. He looked handsome and young in the open casket for his eighty years on this earth.

There is a burial ground for the house slaves near the "Big House," and although most of the wooden grave markers have rotted away, the many depressions in the earth tell of multiple past burials. One special

Bethel AME Church. Georgetown, South Carolina. *Postcard collection, courtesy of Ed Carter.*

one that remains is simple brick and carved stone, which reads simply: "Jane." She was a favorite nurse for the children and grandchildren of the Withers-Forster family. No last name was recorded.

Another burial ground is a half mile beyond the street, and families whose people lived at Friendfield still come from cities like Buffalo, New York, to bury their dead near their ancestors. Until recently, personal items like spectacles and shaving mugs were left on the graves for the use of their owners in the Promised Land, and many names are the same as those of the cabin dwellers from my early days at the plantation. Here are the names of some of the folks who lived in the cabins scattered throughout the place from 1920 to 1950:

> *Henry and Sadie Holmes, James and Rose Graham, Tom and Dollie Joyner, Rosa Johnson, Henry and Hester Green, Henry and Essie Smith, Frank Smith, Levi Holmes, Harper Wineglass, Joe Auiles, David and Frances Nettles, James and Emma McCray, Paul McCray, James McCray Jr., Wesley Bright, Isaac and Sally Reed, Robert and Ola Green, Ella Gallant, Isaiah and Harriet Holmes, Everlena Smith, Mack Wineglass and Gilbert Fulton.*

I loved to go to the little whitewashed church to listen to the singing, clapping and praising Jesus that went along with the fervent praying. Once when I was about ten years old, they asked me to read a Bible verse from the pulpit, which I

In a 1914 photograph from Belle Baruch's scrapbook, kept as a teenager, Jim Powell, head superintendent, and Lucy (McCants or McCray) receive a bounty of bass at the Hobcaw dock. The boys were often engaged to supply fish for the plantation dinners. *Courtesy of the Belle W. Baruch Foundation.*

did—proudly. At that time many of the adults were illiterate, and it was unusual for a "young'un" to be able to read. The little group of people clapped for me, and chorused, "Amen!"—the usual response of affirmation.

These traditional services were called "Sing, Shout and Praise" meetings. The accompaniment to the songs (not called hymns) was a complex, rhythmic, contrapuntal hand clapping and foot stomping. The shouting was a testimonial to Jesus. There often was a tambourine, rarely a piano, and the religious fervor often caused one or two in the female congregation to be seized by the spirit. These ladies would swoon and they had to be supported and fanned by some of the sisters.

The sermons delivered at top volume by the all-powerful preacher were hellfire and damnation, and you had to be pretty confident that you weren't a sinner to hold up your head when on the receiving end. Once I was at Easter service on Sandy Island, and when the gigantic perspiring preacher descended from the pulpit shouting his admonitions and warnings, I felt irretrievably destined to everlasting fiery punishment.

The women sit on one side of the aisle, the important deacons on the other and the rest of the congregation behind. The solemn little children, dressed in their Sunday best, behave beautifully and the women wear lavishly decorated hats. Specially designated sisters wear white dresses, and the ladies of the choir wear matching robes.

Hobcaw Barony. *Postcard collection, courtesy of Ed Carter.*

I always looked forward to attending the South Carolina AME and Baptist Church services, where I have been made to feel welcome with the utmost courtesy. The heartfelt singing by the male and female choir of as many as forty souls and the children's choir—"Buds of Promise"—is an always uplifting joy. In those days, my children and I often attended the New Providence Baptist Church near Pawleys's Island. Peter Small, the butler who succeeded Drayton, was the senior deacon, and he arranged for a special "program" to be incorporated into the service. There were solo and choir Gospel singers, and music that had us jumping in the aisles. In those days you had to walk up to the pulpit with your offering. After everyone had donated, the money was totaled then and there under the watchful eyes of the deacons and the amount was announced: "Fo' dollars and twenty-one cents." The first two counts were never deemed sufficient, and everyone had to divvy up again.

Later, my kids always said, "If our church was like that, we'd go every Sunday!"

The sincere belief in Jesus and the promise of the hereafter gave the African Americans hope and solace when life was hard and there was little to be thankful for. The funerals are moving testimonials of faith. They are called "home going" services—a lovely idea for welcoming the deceased.

Bernard Baruch, Camden native and Wall Street millionaire, was the first Northerner to purchase a winter retreat in Georgetown County, leading the way for an influx of new owners. He wrote in his autobiography that he had hunted all over the world and yet had never found a place equal in wildlife and sport to Hobcaw Barony. He hunted up until the year of his death at age ninety-four. *Courtesy of the Belle W. Baruch Foundation.*

It is a mistake for whites to attend black church services only to look upon them as pageantry or theatre. This is missing the point of their sincerity and belief in the power of Jesus. Church is real, and salvation *is* possible.

I had no understanding back then about the harsh rules of segregation, except when I wasn't allowed to have one of my "colored" friends from the street to the "Big House" for a meal. I could invite a girlfriend in to play jacks, but when lunch came she would slip away to the kitchen, where I would join her after eating in the dining room. We both accepted this as normal.

Much more puzzling was when I wasn't allowed to bring a black playmate with me to the beach at Pawley's Island. I learned later that "colored" people were actually banned from that beach in the mid-1930s. I made a big fuss, because this directly affected my own plans to have a friend to play with, but to no avail. Why? It didn't make sense to me, but again, my little friend accepted the decision without argument and we drove off without her.

I remember once a guest made a disparaging remark about the house servants. She said loudly at the dinner table, "I wonder if we smell as bad to them as they do to us." I blushed furiously and ducked my head

Belle Baruch was an internationally competitive rider and won over 300 awards in Grand Prix jumping, steeplechasing and dressage in Italy, Germany and France. She was fearless and often the only American and the only woman in competition. She retired from riding in 1937 and moved permanently to Hobcaw Barony. By 1956, she owned all of Hobcaw's 17,500 acres and at her early death in 1964, created a trust for the preservation of the land and dedicated its use to research and education in forest and marine sciences. The land today is owned by the Belle W. Baruch Foundation, a private nonprofit organization. *Courtesy of the Belle W. Baruch Foundation.*

to hide hot, quick tears, so afraid that our dear butler Drayton or Miss Liza might have overheard and had their feelings hurt. These and other incidents started me off on a lifelong resentment of racism and snobbery.

But every return visit, since my memories of the old place began, brings a renewal of old sentiments, an appreciation of new pleasures and new insights into the limitations and strengths of Southern culture.

In the mid-1970s I lived for a time in the village of Epulu in central Congo (then Zaire). I was struck by the similarities between culture there and South Carolina black culture as I remembered it from my youth: the same good-hearted hospitality, the same humor and laughter, the same non-crying babies, the same pleasure taken in small things, the same gracious politeness and uncritical acceptance of life. This attitude was due to isolation and ignorance of possibilities, but the intrinsic good nature of most of the Southern blacks I know remains constant.

On the plantation, mysterious noises suffuse the night. Once, the mournful, strident screams of our resident peacock, George, scared me

A young great horned owl being fed. *Courtesy of Frances Cheston Train.*

awake. That year, he was lonesome for his mate, who was probably eaten as she sat on their eggs. During mating season, the resonant courtship calls of great horned owls' mournful "whoo-whoo, whoo-whooing" haunts the dusky dark. Shadows of the waving moss make shifting, suggestive patterns on the moonlit lawn, and I imagine the great black shapes of feral hogs as they make their way up from the marsh to root in the soft sand of the gardens.

Our houseman, rascally Fraser, had formerly worked at the neighboring plantation Hobcaw Barony, owned by Bernard Baruch. Fraser told me that "Capt'n" Baruch kept pet horned owls that walked up and down the steps like little old men. I would have loved to see that!

Fraser was a character much appreciated for his storytelling gifts. One day Pat ordered him to go out to the rice field bank along the river to watch out for poachers. After a morning's patrol, he reported importantly to my father, "Boss, I done catched dem two bad mens who was after yo' ducks, and I got deh names right hyar."

"Good work," said Daddy, pulling out pencil and pad, "We'll get the Law on dem. Tell me who they are."

"Well, Suh one say he Mr. Esso, and other say he name Mr. Mobil." And that ended that, except for the oft-repeated tale.

A nest of turtle eggs. The nest held 175 eggs. *Courtesy of Dr. H.M. Huck's family collection and the Georgetown County Museum.*

The little owlets, looking like balls of gray fluff, often fell from their nests, and restoring them to their homes meant having to climb up onto the precarious last rung of the tallest extension ladder to reach the nest. Once, while on this rescue mission, our present manager Virgil Dugan was struck on the back of his neck by one of the adult owls. He was knocked off the ladder and the claw wounds required six stitches.

Another time, an adult owl became annoyed at me when I ventured too close under the tree where the little owls were staring down at me. I heard a loud clacking noise, and saw the big mother owl advancing across the field toward me on clawed feet, feathers puffed out to create the look of a giant gargoyle, snapping her beak and glaring with malevolent yellow eyes. I didn't wait around to see what she might do next.

An alligator measuring seven feet in length. *Courtesy of Dr. H.M. Huck's family collection and the Georgetown County Museum.*

Silver Hill. *Courtesy of Frances Cheston Train.*

When I was a teenager, I tried to keep a baby owl as a pet. I was a poor mouser, and only managed to trap about three of the mice in our corncrib. These I dangled by their tails over the owlet's head as I imagined a parent owl might do. *SNAP! GULP!* The mice vanished, with only a little bit of one mouse's tail dangling from the owlet's beak. I couldn't catch any more

Silver Hill under construction in 2002. *Courtesy of Frances Cheston Train.*

mice, so the next day I contrived to mold raw hamburger on the end of a string. After the gulp, the string was pulled out, and my invention solved the feeding problem! My pet owl survived well until his wings fledged out, and then we turned him loose.

The poetic sweetness of the Carolina Lowcountry landscape and the sounds of my childhood there still resonate today—the birdsong, the nightly shrilling of tree frogs, the chuckling, quacking voices of coots and duck, the croaks of the heron and the booming of bullfrogs in the marsh. Sometimes I am awakened by the distant barking of the bird dogs and hounds in their kennels as they alert us to the passing of a predator. Gators still patrol the rice fields, and in the spring they bellow and roar as they search for a mate. One night I caught a gator in the beam of my flashlight as I walked along the rice field bank in the dark. His eyes gleamed red as coals as he cruised silently in the ditch canal. They have a mirror-like membrane behind the eyeball that enhances their night vision.

In March and April, the black tannic water reflects azaleas, confederate jasmine, wisteria and cascading Cherokee roses. The graceful blue heron spears fish there, cronking harshly as he flaps away. He and the snowy egret are the loveliest birds with the ugliest voices. A prehistoric-looking anhinga roosts on a low branch, drying his black outstretched wings. He looks at me with his beady eyes and takes to

Children. *Courtesy of the Georgetown County Museum.*

the water like a pterodactyl reincarnated. His long slender neck and rapier-like bill gave him the well-chosen name of "snake bird." Egrets are locally called "Po' Joe's" (no good to eat).

On the plantation there was always something interesting and exciting to do, and we made up our own fun. The derelict house—Silver Hill, originally Mount Pleasant—loomed high in the barnyard. It was a big, square, three-story building made of weathered, unpainted pine and supported by tall brick pillars. It was nearly totally dark inside because the windows were boarded up with plywood, and the wide pine boards were loose and dangerous on the upper floors. My playmates and I bet that we would be brave enough to spend the night inside among the huge field rats and the bats and spiders. Naturally the grown-ups could offer us large rewards with perfect safety, for they knew that we would be far too chicken-hearted to last more than about half an hour after dark.

The old abandoned house was later identified as a 1794 mansion with lovely proportioned rooms, fourteen-foot ceilings and carved cornices and fireplaces. Plantation slaves, who were skilled carpenters and bricklayers,

James Graham, a true gentleman and a man who valued humor and loyalty. His picture now hangs in the gun room. *Courtesy of Frances Cheston Train.*

Mother and friends with Spanish moss beards. *Courtesy of Frances Cheston Train.*

built the house for Robert Withers, a son of the first owner of Friendfield. It remained unoccupied after his death in 1830. Silver Hill is the only existing example of a plantation house built in the vernacular in our region of the Lowcountry that had not been modified in any way since the eighteenth century—no additions, plumbing or electricity. It was a forgotten building and wasn't listed on the tax rolls—a fact my father did not hasten to correct.

A plantation Christmas party for the children of the workers used to be held at Silver Hill every year, and "Sandy Claw" doled out the gifts that had been individually wrapped by our manager's wife, Jessie, who called each child by name to come forward to receive the oranges and toys. She told me she had to wrap at least a dozen extra for all their friends and relations who had a way of showing up for the party. The rest of the time the old house stayed empty, used only to store hay and scrap lumber.

Belle Baruch, *far right*, entertained many of her schoolmates during the early 1900s, as evidenced by this circa 1916 photograph taken at Clambank Landing's hunt cabin, overlooking North Inlet estuary. *Courtesy of the Belle W. Baruch Foundation.*

It has now been meticulously restored to its former splendor by my ex-son-in-law, Daniel Thorne, under the expert supervision of Tommy Graham, a well-known master of historic preservation techniques. Back then we only thought of it as our old wreck of a haunted house.

Friendfield was where I saw my father most. Being the youngest child, I could skip a few weeks of school on each end of regular vacations. He helped me (impatiently) with my hated math workbooks, and took me on long tramps through the rice fields on the muddy dikes. He identified the birds and ducks for me, and we were both keenly interested in the moccasins, gators, fiddler crabs and bullfrogs. We were good companions in those days.

Everyone respected my father but we were all scared of him. We never could get away with a thing. The men said, "De Boss eye so keen, he can spot a gnat on an orange across de yard." When he walked in the rice fields, loyal Drayton had to follow him out to the marsh—still wearing his butler's white coat and black trousers—with a silver tray bearing the glass of milk that my father was supposed to drink every two hours. That was the diet for ulcers then: creamed food and rich milk. It was a prescription that eventually contributed to his heart disease and strokes.

Out hunting, my father always wore a twill jacket, a tweed woolen necktie, a neat woolen shirt and greased, knee-high, Gokey snake-proof boots. James

Wedgefield Plantation. *Courtesy of the Georgetown County Museum.*

Graham, the dog handler, always maintained, "De boss must have been some kin' of sargint in de war, on account he alway dress so neat."

One time James shared the front seat of the pickup with my father and Pat on the long trip to the upcountry shoot. This was unusual, and James found himself wedged in between Pat and Daddy. He had a huge wad of Red Dog chewing tobacco in his cheek and nowhere to spit, being too intimidated to ask them to stop the car so he could get out. He got sicker and sicker, and he told me later: "I was too glad I be a color' man, so de Boss couldn't see me greenin' up. I like to bust wide open before we arrive. Ooh, I was *too* sick!"

Another time, again riding upcountry, James had a bad headache and Pat gave him an Alka-Seltzer. He didn't know you had to drop the tablet in a glass of water, so "I jus' chew it up and pretty soon it commence to fizz, and the fizz come out my nose and my mout' and my ear." James had a wonderful sense of humor and he relished a joke—even if it was on himself.

My mother loved to laugh with the men, and they reminisce about the time they were watching her have her picture taken with three of her proper lady houseguests, all sitting seriously on the front porch wearing full beards of Spanish moss. She was never above giving them a complicit

Windsor Plantation. *Courtesy of the Georgetown County Museum.*

wink when Daddy was scolding them about something. She loved the story about the time Pat was talking to old Isaiah Holmes and a plane happened to fly overhead. It was a rare occurrence in the 1930s and in those days everyone looked up when they heard a plane. Pat asked him, "What do you think of airplanes, Isaiah?" Isaiah thought about it, scratched his head and said, "I tell you de trut Capt'n Pat, I now be haf daid, and when I gets took to de sky, I don' want to be broke up wid some air crash. When years pass all de white folks be up in de air, and all the black folks will hab de hiway to deyselves."

The house parties in those days when I was little were great fun and I could hear the grown-ups' laughter echoing from the dining room all the way back to my nursery wing. Many guests came from Philadelphia and New York. The men were all quail and duck hunters, and their wives were sporty types who enjoyed the life. Looking through the guest book I see the signatures of many perennials like the Watson Webbs. Mr. Webb was sour and grumpy, and his wife Electra was a dedicated, pioneering collector of American folk art. They were both wonderful shots. Mrs. Webb even held the record for a giant Kodiak bear. Cousin Livingston

Mansfield Plantation. *Courtesy of the Georgetown County Museum.*

Biddle wrote long complementary verses in the guest book. My family's best friend, Mr. Kline, was a yearly visitor. We children loved Mr. Francis Richmond—a bachelor with a loud, jolly haw-haw laugh—who used to get down on the floor and play raucous games of "Pit" with us, luring us into the forbidden parlor.

Mr. Charlie Cadwalader came every year. He was supposed to be on the wagon but managed to pour half a decanter of sherry in his turtle soup. Mr. Robert Goelet got tipsy and wrote suggestive remarks to my mother in the guest book. Tall, awkward Mr. Joe Lippincott, the Philadelphia publisher, collected tree snail shells at his home on Casey Key, and kept pet crows at his home in Philadelphia. He gave me one named Joe Crow and told me a funny story about how one of his crows hated his mother-in-law and used to glide silently down behind her when she was drinking iced tea on the porch and peck her ankles.

Mr. Arthur Meigs, the short-tempered architect of the Friendfield restoration, was an annual visitor, and was not so secretly in love with my mother. She enjoyed the attention but never reciprocated, as was the frustrating case for all her admirers. Another of these was Mr. George

Rice Hope Plantation. *Courtesy of the Georgetown County Museum.*

Widener, who remained devoted until her death. I remember he called on her after her stroke and I saw tears in his eyes when I gave him the message from my bedridden mother that, "I don't want him to see me when I am like this." He left the house bowed with grief.

My family had many friends who owned neighboring plantations, but they would usually only visit for lunch or cookouts in the woods before the quail hunts, as the driving distances were too great. At that time, in the 1930s, Yankees like Mr. and Mrs. DuPont of Kinlaw Plantation; our cousins Paul and Lalla Mills of Windsor Plantation; Colonel and Mrs. Robert Montgomery of Mansfield; Mr. and Mrs. Robert Goelet of Wedgefield; Mr. and Ms. Billy Beach of Rice Hope; the Oliver Iselins of Venture; Mrs. Emerson, from Cliffton; George Vanderbilt of Arcadia; George Legendre from Medway; and the Guggenheims of Cain Hoy had bought up many of the old places, rescuing them from decrepitude. My parents' great friends, the Nick Roosevelts, owners of Gippy Plantation, were an exception—after all she was a Sinkler from Charleston and not an arriviste Northerner!

There was no money in the South after the Civil War, and the locals didn't resent the newcomers as deeply as you might think. They loved their

Bernard Baruch entertained presidents, congressmen, men in the military, industry, journalism and music professions, as well as world leaders such as Winston Churchill. In a photo taken on the dock at Hobcaw Barony in January 1932, Belle Baruch and her father, Bernard, welcome Churchill and his daughter, Diana, for several days' visit on the plantation. The Churchills traveled by yacht, motoring up from the Bahamas. Churchill was recuperating from a December traffic accident in New York City, which had occurred as he made his way to Bernard Baruch's Fifth Avenue home for dinner one evening. He recovered and went on to serve as England's prime minister. The rest he found at Hobcaw may have changed world events. *Courtesy of the Belle W. Baruch Foundation.*

homeland and were pleased that the old places were being saved because it was impossible in those hard times for the original owners to keep them up. The Yankee presence brought in new money and created jobs in that

Tom Joyner, the huntsman. *Courtesy of Frances Cheston Train.*

Kaminski's residence. Georgetown, South Carolina. *Postcard collection, courtesy of Ed Carter.*

Waterfront. Georgetown, South Carolina. *Postcard collection, courtesy of Ed Carter.*

depressed rural community. Now, fifty years later, the situation is reversed and the plantations are once more owned and enjoyed by Southerners, or have been made into golf courses and gated communities.

In 1932, Winston Churchill visited his old friend Bernard Baruch at nearby Hobcaw Barony, and a luncheon was given for him at which the champagne flowed. My parents were invited and Mummy was seated next to Churchill. He was at his amusing best, and she was entranced. She avoided Daddy's eye and his broad hints that it was time to go home. The brandy made its rounds, prolonging the lunch—to the annoyance

Another view of the Georgetown waterfront. *Courtesy of the Caledonia Plantation Collection and the Georgetown County Museum.*

of my teetotal father. Afterwards he remained personally skeptical about Churchill for a long time, until World War II changed his opinion. "Damn drunk," Daddy said, dismissing the great man. Was he jealous? I suppose so, although it was not the first time my mother had captivated a man at a party.

Another famous visitor to Hobcaw was President Franklin D. Roosevelt. His private railroad car was scheduled to drop him off at the Atlantic Coastline Railroad spur that passed by the front gate of Friendfield.

Tom Joyner the huntsman happened to be riding his bike down the driveway when, "All dem army mens in uniform popped out de bushes, and dey order me to hol' up me hans and stop right there. I thought sho' enough the War had dun come to Georgetown!"

According to local gossip, on one of his trips Mr. Roosevelt brought along a guest, Lucy Mercer Rutherford, who was officially Mrs. Roosevelt's secretary at the White House, but also President Roosevelt's mistress in her spare time. A few days later, Eleanor Roosevelt paid a surprise visit. Supposedly, Mrs. Rutherford was rushed out the back door just as the first lady arrived at the front, and scandal was averted.

In the spring, three or four of the shooting ponies were moved down to the small, whitewashed stable near the marsh and cypress swamp at the far end of the lawn. My friends and I were allowed to ride by ourselves, but catching the ponies in the corral was a hard job. The little horses were pigheaded and wheeled away from us, kicking up puffs of sand and dust. They hated opening their mouths for the bit and would clench their long yellow teeth, and we were too short to force the bridle up over their pinned back ears.

Just as we despaired, kindly James Graham, who was watching out for us all the time, came to the rescue. The minute the horses saw him shaking a pan of oats, they would become tractable, and he saddled them up for us, tightening the girths with mighty heaves as the ponies tried to swell up their stomachs against the constricting pressure.

Off we trotted from the corral, cap pistols at the ready, armed to the teeth with rolls of red caps that smelled pungently of gunpowder when we fired at each other. We cantered along sandy roads through the woods, the green tops of the pines contrasting with a blue Carolina sky. The sun was warm on our backs, yellow and blue butterflies fluttered over bright green ferns, purple violets and wild flag and the unshod hooves of our horses plopped softly in the sand.

A favorite destination was Tompkins Store next to the highway, about a mile down the front drive. It was a ramshackle frame building and a rusty, tin "Drink Coca-Cola" sign flapped lopsidedly above the front porch. A few old white men sat outside on wooden kitchen chairs, "a-whittlin' and a-spittin'," and after they watched us tie up the ponies to spindly gum trees, they returned to their pastime without comment, aside from a "How you'all?" and a wave.

Inside there was a beat-up wooden counter and a few stools, presided over by red-faced, bristly Mr. Tompkins, who leaned over to beam down on us with rheumy eyes, spraying us with his pungent breath. "What'll be your pleasure, little lady? Great God, almighty, ain't you all sumpin' to be ridin' all this way from home. Mighty glad to greet you on this lovely day!"

We drank warmish sodas from murky Coca-Cola glasses, feeling very independent as we searched for the coins to pay. Then, *ZAP!* Without warning and to our everlasting astonishment, Mr. Tompkins squirted a juicy jet of dark brown tobacco juice across the counter. It landed with an accurate pinging splat into the brass spittoon in the corner, just missing my head on its way.

Now we understood the full richness of a favorite jingle sung to the aria from *Carmen*: "Toreador-a, don't spit on the floor, use the cuspidor, that's what it's for."

"You'all hurry back now, you hear?" drawled Mr. T. and we rode on back home, practicing our hawking and messy spitting amid gales of giggles.

Another expedition was the ride to the foundation of an old abandoned menhaden processing plant—"The Fish Factory"—which was flooded with river water and covered with bright green algae scum. One time two huge alligators were trapped in there near a half-submerged, bloated, hairy carcass of a deer. They floated on the surface with just their snouts and eye ridges showing. The smell was sickening. We threw in a branch and the gators dove with a terrifying *WHUMP!* of their scaly tails. The horses shied and tried to bolt, and we fled for our lives.

The iron mouths of the ponies never responded to the fiercest sawing tugs, and almost always one of the ponies ran away—to its rider's dismay—on the way home. Normally they were only ridden in the winter for quail shooting, hardly ever going faster than a walk, and so they took clever advantage of our inept horsemanship and tore back to the barn. They hadn't finished shedding their winter coats yet, and the sweat foamed up under the girths and gobs of hair stuck to the wet saddle blankets.

We arrived back at the stables breathless and scared that we would get into trouble with Mummy and Daddy, who had ordered us never to bring the ponies home hot. But James never told on us, and the ponies didn't seem to be the worse for it.

We left the blankets and tack to dry on the corral fence and came back to the house, smelling pungently of horse. We were dirty, hot, and excited to relate the various happenings on the ride—getting "lost," nearly falling off, maybe sighting a snake or a hawk or a wild pig and being scared to death by the gators.

# CHAPTER 5

# Plantation Management

Timber harvesting—now the chief source of our plantation revenue—has always been carefully controlled, and areas are selectively cut each summer. The entire upland property is burned over each spring to keep down the undergrowth and litter; fire lines are ploughed; and the land is managed for quail and wildlife propagation. If the litter and brush were left unchecked, hunting dogs and shooting ponies couldn't travel through the woods, and the lespedeza and millet patches that attract the wild quail could not be planted. Longleaf pine is fire resistant, so the burning process does not damage this valuable crop.

It is much harder to manage a large hunting preserve today than it was the past—in spite of the use of modern agricultural machinery—and it has become vastly more expensive. There are myriad regulations to contend with concerning pesticides and endangered species—no more shooting the blue darter when he swoops down on a plump quail or killing that gator when you catch him on the lawn trying to hypnotize the puppy. The skins are very valuable in fact, and when they were protected, a boot maker or handbag designer had to pay up to a thousand dollars for a perfect skin from a gator of just the right age. The tanning process is very long and the dyeing and styling are complicated and technically demanding.

Now, in 2007, bald eagles and red-cockaded woodpeckers are also making a big comeback. We have had a nesting pair of eagles for years and monitor about nine colonies of the valuable woodpeckers, whose territory is shrinking due to the progressive loss of suitable pine forests. The U.S. Fish and Wildlife Service decreed that each colony ensures a protected area of between sixty and seventy acres. If you identify extra colonies, you can trap one to sell for large amounts of money to a

The front gate at Litchfield Plantation. *Postcard collection, courtesy of Ed Carter.*

property that doesn't have any. Some estimate that there are only four to five thousand family units left in the whole Southern territory.

The red-cockaded woodpecker is a tiny bird, five to seven inches long, with a nearly invisible red "cockade"—more like a tiny stripe on his head. He has a nasty, strident cry and excavates a cavity in a living pine tree, usually a longleaf, to make a nest site. This wounds the tree, and is easily identified by a long white stripe of sap running down the bark. The sticky sap inhibits the predatory rat snake from climbing up to devour the baby woodpeckers or eggs—a favorite food.

Today, a regulation that complicates the process of burning by permit is making wildlife management more difficult. In the days before this law, it took only five days to burn the entire upland property; now, it usually takes about twenty. Each burn must have its own permit based on wind direction, velocity and humidity. If smoke should blow from the plantation across Highway 521, it might be blamed for an accident and we would risk a lawsuit. We must also consider the Harmony development across the river from us when the wind is blowing in that direction. Everyone connected with the burn must be experienced and alert during the burning, and afterward must watch out for those pine stumps that can smolder on for days. "Outing stumps" takes a long time.

Constant monitoring of the quail and turkey population is part of the manager's job. Wild quail have declined on Friendfield due to

Quail shooting with Pat McClary in the front. *Courtesy of Frances Cheston Train.*

A picnic lunch on the Sampit River before quail shooting. *Courtesy of Frances Cheston Train.*

A successful fox hunt. *Courtesy of the Caledonia Plantation Collection and the Georgetown County Museum.*

their loss of habitat—the small farms where they used to forage on the fringes of orchards and planted fields. Hurricane Hugo devastated the natural population of wild birds, and on our plantation they never quite recovered. Hunting pressure has necessitated putting out pen-raised quail, which do not breed in the wild. There are various theories—stationary feeders, broadcast feed stations, putting out just-hatched babies—and the experiments go on and on.

One thing that has been proven is that these food places attract snakes and hawks that soon know where their grocery store is located. Another predator is the fire ants that swarm over the baby wild quail as soon as they are hatched, still wet from the egg.

My family's life on the plantation was centered on hunting quail, ducks, deer and turkey within their respective seasons. Often, in earlier days, fox hunts started before dawn. James or Tom stationed one of us on a farm road, where we waited for the fox at a likely crossing. After what seemed like hours in the cold, breaking day—nothing. Finally, we would hear the stirring sound of the fox and deerhounds in full, joyous cry back in the piney woods. "They've jumped him!" would sound a faraway shout. If he trotted across the road within range of our ambush, we were supposed to shoot him with a shotgun. Luckily, I never was in the right place. I couldn't have done the deed, but it was believed to be necessary to get rid of the foxes and bobcats that were supposedly prime quail predators. They were tricky those gray foxes, and often climbed a tree to escape the relentless pursuit of the hounds. There was also coon hunting, wild

Fox hunting on the Waccamaw Neck was a frequent pleasure for the Baruchs and their guests at Hobcaw. Belle Baruch was an avid huntswoman and was a member of the hunt in Pau, France; Bedford, New York; and Middleburg, Virginia. She described foxhunting on DeBordieu Island, where owner Mrs. Isaac Emerson offered her party refreshments and on Caledonia and Waverly plantations where Ralph Nesbit directed his black staff to prepare "the fluffiest omelets ever" for Belle and her hunting party. Note the mid-nineteenth-century rice barge being utilized for the return of the horses. *Courtesy of the Belle W. Baruch Foundation.*

boar hunting and, of course, deer hunting. Everyone loved to hunt, and watching the expert skinning process after the requisite hanging period was something that always fascinated me.

Hunting deer with a pack of hounds is now illegal. People of Pat's generation lived for that sport from September to January. Nowadays, deer hunting is done from stands, and most of the hunters are after trophy heads so it doesn't seem to cut back on the excess doe population. Hunting is considered a good way to teach a child, maybe as young as seven, how to handle a rifle. Sitting high up there in the tree stand on Daddy's lap, trembling with excitement, sighting his or her kid-size rifle on that first buck—there is no better way to bond with Daddy, Southern style. You get your shirttail cut off as proud proof to show your success when you got home.

We were never in Carolina during good striper or spot tail fishing season, something I've always regretted. I did hook onto a big catfish once, sitting on the bank of our island in the rice field with my father,

Clyde Steamship Company. *Postcard collection, courtesy of Ed Carter.*

casting out into the Sampit. I remember praying, "Please God, and don't let me lose it. I'll do anything, please!" And my father, stern as usual, remonstrated: "God doesn't like to be bothered with little things like that. Someday, when it's really important, he'll remember: oh its just that same kid again who wanted to catch an old catfish, and he'll turn a deaf ear."

One day, fly casting in the rice field on Annadale Plantation, my small grandson made a wrong cast into a ditch behind him. Believe it or not a flounder leapt out of the water and grabbed his fly. It was the only fish he caught, except for a couple of spots, and we grilled them on the beach at Huntington State Park. Ever after our tale was of "Thomas and the Killer Flounder."

Another memorable—if unorthodox—fish was a beautiful shining sea trout that was purloined by my resourceful Jack Russell terrier from some hapless fisherman's cooler on the south end of the beach at Pawleys, near the creek outlet. We called and called, and finally Schnapps came trotting back to the car, a trout still flapping in his jaws. He jumped in, and we were too embarrassed to go looking for the fisherman to confess the crime. We ate it for dinner, and never was there a more delicious fish.

In the heyday of rice growing the white owners never stayed on the plantations during the suffocating heat of the summer. They packed up and traveled to their beach houses, or to the mountains where it was

A.C. Lumber Company. *Postcard collection, courtesy of Ed Carter.*

healthier. They left the overseer, usually a white man, to run the property. I used to think that this would be hard on the managers, but actually it gave them freedom to run the place the way they wanted without too much interference from the Yankee boss who often was ignorant or dismissive of Southern customs and culture.

Pat used to hate it when Daddy returned from the Plantation Society meetings "full of damn fool ideas." He claimed that the owners always wanted to try out new theories, which any native-born Southerner just plain knew wouldn't work—seed that wouldn't grow in our climate, cattle that would get hoof rot in the marshy fields, shooting ponies that were too tall or too well-bred to follow along quietly, plants for the garden that deer would devour as soon as they pricked above the ground. Soybeans were one such futile attempt in our area. After the first years of big success, farmers "planted the sidewalks," as the saying goes, and the price plummeted. My father's conviction was that he would never get into agriculture. "Stick to timber" he advised. "That's what this soil and climate grow best—pine trees."

I think my father must have made Pat's life miserable, for he was the micromanager type of absentee owner. He checked up on every detail by phone and letter from Philadelphia. I remember Pat telling me incredulously that he got a phone call asking to know how many nails a certain repair job had actually required before he paid the bill for a pound

Virgil Dugan, Friendfield's manager (1971–present). *Courtesy of Frances Cheston Train.*

of nails. He hoped and expected there would be some left over and please to let him know by return mail. All plantation bills were sent to his office and checks were signed by Daddy personally.

He also did most of the housekeeping. I have a list in Daddy's angular script spelling out the details: windows shut and locked, blinds pulled down, cover chandeliers, remove light bulbs, close dampers, rugs rolled up with camphor balls, loose cushions put in cedar room, bathroom curtains taken off rods and laid flat on beds under covers, rugs and carpets that can't be rolled covered with moth balls, cover lampshades and paintings, linen washed and put away, gin and whisky locked in cellar, thoroughly clean kitchen, pantry storeroom rid of all food, Mr. and Mrs. Cheston's clothes packed neatly in trunks, all blankets and quilts in boxes in cedar room, soap from bathrooms put away in boxes and the list goes on.

Also stored in the attic cedar room were reams and reams of toilet paper packed in sturdy cardboard boxes that my father must have hoarded before the war, fearing a shortage. These supplies were slipped into special wooden holders that were screwed on the wall next to all the toilets. The tan, five- by seven-inch sheets were about as absorbent as wax paper, glossy and shiny, with darker colored flecks of splinters. He was hellbent that we use them all up, and there they stayed for years, much to the distress and amusement of guests and family. He resented the rolls of nice, white absorbent paper that we preferred, and lived on in the vain hope that somehow his purchase would be justified.

In the case of Friendfield's managers, we have been more than fortunate. Pat McClary, 1930 to 1972, was a unique and memorable fixture during the lifetime of my parents until his retirement. He was followed by another unusually competent and intelligent character, Virgil Dugan, from the time of Pat's retirement until the present.

Virgil is a handsome and athletic man. He has only one arm but he can accomplish more physical things than any two-handed man I know. He can saddle and bridle a horse, play left-handed golf with a seven handicap and is a crack shot with shotgun and rifle. He is a fund of knowledge on wildlife matters and thinks like a lawyer, with a well considered, experienced answer or opinion on everything. He has a fiendish sense of humor and a vast repertoire of practical jokes and stories.

When Virgil first came to Friendfield he wore a fake arm, a rather corpse-like prosthesis with creepy, outstretched fingers that he has long since abandoned. My children liked to think that he had been the victim of an alligator with a grudge, like Captain Hook's crocodile, but he actually lost it in an accident with a hydraulic press at age eighteen. One day, my daughter Frances and two friends were riding their ponies out on the rice field dike with Virgil leading the expedition. Suddenly he called out, "Whoa, hold up, don't move." He jumped off his horse, reached down into the reeds and pulled out a long, shiny cottonmouth moccasin, gripping it behind the head so that the fangs were exposed. The girls screamed as the snake buried its fangs onto his bare "arm." He let it hang there a moment and then flung it back into the river. They were naturally horrified and did not guess that he had shot the snake earlier that morning, and that his arm was the fake one.

Virgil knows everyone in Georgetown and is immeasurably helpful and tuned in to local politics. When the state of South Carolina wanted to route a major highway right through the heart of the plantation and build a bridge across the Sampit in front of Silver Hill, he was able to thwart the plan by drawing attention to a bald eagle nesting site right in the proposed path.

He is a tough man but he is devoted to Friendfield. We are lucky that he is on our team for he would make a formidable opponent. Both he and Pat were and are blessed with extraordinary wives: Jessie Vereen McClary and Virginia Dugan. Their patient understanding of their strong-willed, hot-tempered husbands created long-term, stable marriages and fine children and grandchildren—all of them part of the Friendfield heritage.

# Chapter 6

# Hunting Tales

The night coon hunt was our favorite adventure of all. After supper—which for once, we were allowed to eat without changing out of blue jeans—we were boosted into the back of Pat's pickup and went jouncing off into the mysterious dark.

A bright moon pooled brilliant white light on the forest floor between the etched black shadows of the live oaks. The hounds were released from their cages in the back of the dog truck and went crashing off toward the Port's Creek swamp, sounding a confused medley of barks and yips and deep-throated howls. The air smelled of pine, mud and wildness, and the men whooped and hollered encouragement to their dogs: "Speak to him, Rock!" or Stranger or Queenie, or whichever hound belonged to him. "Listening at de dawgs" was like hearing an unfolding story. Some hounds were silent trailers until they barked "treed," and others bayed as soon as they struck a hot trail. The men knew each dog's voice individually, which stage of the chase he was signaling and what type of game he was trailing, and they likened it to music. It was bad if they ran a deer, because the hounds would seldom obey calls to return, sometimes staying away for days, swimming the creeks and even the river and risking being eaten by the ever-hopeful alligators.

When they struck a fresh scent, Pat blew a long mellow blast on his hunting horn: a cow horn with a bit of hide still on it, and no mouthpiece. None of us could ever make a sound come out of it, even though we blew till our cheeks popped.

Then we were off—running through thorny brush and cane swamp, rubber boots squelching, following the faint light of the lantern or flashlight way ahead. "Don't go that away, that thicket's so thick, a dawg would have to back up to bark! Come around hyar, watch for the ravine."

A lady and gentleman on the hunt. *Courtesy of Dr. H.M. Huck's family collection and the Georgetown County Museum.*

Breathlessly we staggered on, until someone yelled, "He's treed, he's treed!" as the dogs' barking rhythm changed to a sharp frantic staccato. When we caught up, the dogs would be leaping at the tree trunk, trying desperately to climb after their quarry, biting off chunks of bark and looking like mad hounds of hell in the flickering light.

And up there, hunched on a high branch, was the furry masked raccoon, picked out by the beam of a powerful flashlight. "Shine his eyes, shine his eyes!" and his bright little eyes reflected the beam. The designated shooter aimed, while someone shouted "Pop him in de haid." There was a sharp crack of the .22 rifle, a smell of powder and—after a desperate, clinging delay—the doomed coon came crashing down through the branches into the snapping, fighting melee of bloodthirsty hounds.

A hunting party. *Courtesy of the Caledonia Plantation Collection and the Georgetown County Museum.*

After a yell of "Stretch 'im boys" the dogs were whipped off, and the raccoon was dropped into a gunnysack to be skinned and served up for someone's Sunday roast. The hill raccoons that fed on acorns were prized, unlike the carrion-eating possum or the marsh coons that ate fish and frogs.

Another time a coon took refuge in a hollow halfway up a gum tree. "We'll have to smoke him out," said Pat, as the dogs jumped and tore at the bark. "What we goin' smoke him wit?" asked Junior. "Take off your shirt," said Pat, "and climb up there to that holler. Wrap your shirt around this stick and set it afire, and poke it down that hole."

We watched anxiously, as the shirt burned to blackened scraps, the dogs became wild with suspense and nothing emerged. Junior slid back down, shivering in his undershirt. "Grab de axe, boy, and we'll chop her down!" Junior went to work with the axe on the tree trunk and when the tree was nearly severed, Pat—who loved having the last word—demanded the axe and delivered the final mighty *WHACK!* after Junior had done all the work. Out scrambled the coon, slightly singed, into the melee of barking dogs—and that was that. Pat would go to any lengths to capture any game.

On one of the hunts the hounds killed a possum, which was then considered a prime predator against quail. "Look at this," Pat told us, and with a forefinger he scooped seven tiny squirming, hairless, pink babies out of the mother possum's pouch. In front of our horrified eyes, he stepped on them, commenting, "They would have died anyway." This

A little girl with a gun. *Courtesy of Dr. H.M. Huck's family collection and the Georgetown County Museum.*

was hard to take for two Northern girls like my cousin Minnie and me, and we never forgot that shocking moment. Life in the woods, and nature itself, is brutal. "People who talk about the 'Cathedral of the Woods' ain't never been there in real life," an old-timer once told me disgustedly.

Pat's wife Jessie told me that once she and her husband were driving to a wedding, all dressed up. Pat was wearing a white suit, and he spotted a possum by the side of the road. He screeched the car to a halt, grabbed his ever-present rifle, leaped out and shot it, spattering his good clothes with mud and blood. Jessie was appalled and read him the riot act, but nothing ever changed him. Hunting was his passion.

Hobcaw Barony guests, photographed circa 1920, were entertained well by staff, even in the absence of owners Mr. and Mrs. Bernard Baruch. Head superintendent Jim Powell, *holding young child*, and his niece Lois Massey, *far right*, kept a book on each guest to describe their favorite hunting guides, horses and drinks. *Courtesy of the Belle W. Baruch Foundation.*

One big change now from the old days is that everyone born after 1977 has to pass a state hunter-safety course before they are granted a license, but in those days we were brought up around guns, and certainly taught by our dads, older brothers or mentors to respect them and to obey the mandatory safety rules. When we made our expeditions out to the rice fields, orders from the Boss limited us to one gun per group. We were taught to stand behind the designated shooter and take turns.

> *Never fire a rifle up into the air, the bullet can travel a mile and may ricochet. Don't fire flat across the water for the same reason. Don't use your rifle as a walking stick. Be careful no trash falls down the barrel. Never take the safety off until you're ready to fire. At the end of the adventure aim at the ground and pull the trigger at least five times to make certain the gun is empty before returning to the house.*

And so forth. Gun cleaning was a mandatory ritual after each outing.

In the old days I rarely walked out onto the rice field banks without my gun, and my kids did the same. We all started the same way, first with a "Daisy" air rifle—you stored the little cup-shaped lead pellets in your

A circa 1907 deer hunting scene at Hobcaw Barony features guests, plantation managers and African American staff members. Kneeling, with the white beard, is Dr. Simon Baruch, Jewish immigrant, Confederate surgeon and medical pioneer. Kneeling in the foreground is Harry Donaldson, superintendent. Seated on horseback is Bernard Baruch with his daughter, Renee. *Courtesy of the Belle W. Baruch Foundation.*

A good day's hunt. *Courtesy of the Caledonia Plantation Collection and the Georgetown County Museum.*

mouth for quick loading—then a BB gun fired by $CO_2$ cartridges and finally much later, graduating to a .22 rifle (shorts only). I loved the sound of the copper-nosed .22 bullets sliding down the loading tube, and the satisfactory scrunch when you rammed them home. The bullets made a great *THWUNK* when they hit the water, and we shot "at" everything— branches, floating leaves, half submerged logs, little black turtle noses just poking up through the muddy surface water and best of all, fiddler crabs. A direct hit would scatter pieces of the scrabbling critters like broken Ritz crackers. We were forbidden to shoot coots, blackbirds, shorebirds, herons or ducks, and never dared shoot at alligators for fear of provoking them, or snakes unless you could be certain of hitting them in the head.

One time when my son Whitney was about thirteen years old he went out for his first duck hunt and returned for breakfast with a distinctly smug expression. He asked everyone around the table, "How many did you get?" Of course the competition among the teenagers was intense, but one after another the other three hunters confessed to small success— one duck or two or none. "Well," bragged Whit, "I got seven!" They all rushed out to the back porch, unbelieving. He got seven, all right, seven coots! Poor Whit, he never lived it down, and we gave him a little trophy with "Whitney, Coot Shoot Champion" engraved on its plaque. It still sits on the library desk after forty years.

When kids were finally allowed to join in the quail hunt, it was a thrilling day. The young first-time hunter rides out on his pony with the

Sam and Boise inspect the kennels. *Courtesy of the Caledonia Plantation Collection and the Georgetown County Museum.*

rest of the shooting party, following the well-trained bird dogs (pointers or setters) while they search out elusive coveys. The dogs hunt eagerly, ranging far but obeying the shrill whistle of their trainer. Brambles often rip their lolling tongues as they plunge heedlessly in and out of ditches and swamp edge at full run.

Then a pointer freezes, tail stiff, head and nose turned toward the invisible bird. The dog handler yells, "Point!" The teenager leaps off his pony, pulls the shotgun from its scabbard, carefully slips the shells in the chamber, makes sure the safety is on and, trembling with trepidation, walks stealthily up to the pointer, who with eyes bulging, is inhaling the heady smell of quail so intensely that its whole body quivers with suppressed longing. The suspense is heightened if the dogs are not exactly up with the birds, and the hunter follows them, his heart thumping, jumping at each little sound, while they creep along daintily, trailing the birds through the feed patch of lespedeza brush. "Careful, careful, hunt close, hunt close," cautions the handler to his dogs, while at the same time motioning the young hunter not to hang back.

I remember being the cause of much hilarity when one of the ponies sneezed explosively behind me, scaring me half to death. I whirled, and nearly fell down, certain it was a covey rise. Such is the tension in the field.

Captain Foster Bourne shooting. *Courtesy of the Wright-Skinner family collection and the Georgetown County Museum.*

You might think those tiny feathered creatures were tigers the way they can startle you.

Suddenly, always unexpectedly, the covey erupts with a huge whirr of wings, *WHIZZ!*, the little birds fly every which way, and our terrified boy, in desperation, fires into the middle of the flight, forgetting the admonition to pick out one bird and sight on it. Miracle of miracles, a bird falls. "Hunt daid, hunt daid," encourages the handler, and after a long tail-wagging search one of the dogs picks up the dead bird and presents it to the triumphant shooter. This is one of the proudest days a youngster could have. The first quail! A landmark day for a neophyte hunter, and one he will never forget.

In my own case, I was about thirteen years old when I first went into the field with an actual loaded shotgun. I had walked up many times before, practicing with an empty gun, and of course "shooting" lots of birds. Easy! But this test was the real thing, under the watchful eyes of Pat and my father. Trying to absorb all their admonitions and cautionary advice, I failed repeatedly to connect with the zipping birds and the failures were making me gun-shy and nervous.

In an early twentieth-century photograph featuring a fair day's hunt, a hundred ducks brought down in only a few hours in the marshes of Hobcaw lie at the feet of Charlie McCants Sr. and the Caines brothers. Bob, Hucks and Sawney Caines were known as top hunting guides. They lived at Hobcaw and carved the only known South Carolina decoys expressly for use by Bernard Baruch. Those decoys are valuable collectibles today. *Courtesy of the Belle W. Baruch Foundation.*

It was nearing the end of the long afternoon when another whirring covey flew up in a bunch to my left. I froze, and didn't get my gun off. Then, after a pause, a lone quail—a sleeper—flew off in a long sweeping curve to my right. I swung the shotgun a little ahead, and *BANG!*, the quail dropped in a cloud of feathers. My heart was beating a tattoo, and I think I outran the bird dog to the spot where my quail hit down in the broom straw.

It lay dead, and I cried a little when I picked up its warm feathered body. I still remember the enormous pride I felt when my father turned to Pat with a big smile, "She's going to be all right," he said. I was never a very good shot because I lacked the hunter's zeal for killing, but pleasing my father more than made up for my difficulties that day.

The weather in January in the late 1930s seemed to have been much colder than nowadays, and our rice fields were teeming with ducks of all varieties—the big canvas backs and black ducks; ring necks, summer ducks (wood ducks); blue and green winged teal; mallards; shovelers; and pintails—all of them coming in to rest and feed on their way further south.

Boats are necessary equipment in duck hunting. *Courtesy of the Caledonia Plantation Collection and the Georgetown County Museum.*

Around 5:00 a.m. the door to my cold bedroom opened quietly, admitting a shaft of electric light from the hall and the familiar round shape of the chambermaid, Eliza Myers. "Good morning, Miss Frances, time to rise and get you some ducks!"

"No, no," I grumbled, huddling deeper under the cozy quilt, peeking out as she bent and lit a split of fatwood to touch off the fire that had been laid in readiness the night before. She shuffled around the big room in her black felt carpet slippers, raising the blinds to reveal only cold blackness, admonishing, "Hurry now, your Daddy's already downstairs."

Thinking about the duck hunt the night before was exciting, but the getting up part required a degree of zeal, which seemed to have faded during sleep. I draped my long woolen underwear tops and bottoms on the fire screen—barely rescuing them from scorch temperature when the fire crackled into a blaze—and I hopped about trying to pull them on. (Like the old verse, "Liar, Liar, Pants on Fire!") Then came heavy woolen socks, flannel shirt, turtleneck sweater, khaki colored canvas pants—puff, puff, can't button the pants, too many clothes on! Next, a canvas duck-cloth jacket, tan wool scarf, remembered my gloves and more puffing.

Finally downstairs, I ran (waddled) to the gunroom, a masculine business-like room, holding two ancient leather armchairs, shotguns neatly racked, cases of shells—12 gauge and 20s, 4.10s and 16s—stacked under the gun cleaning table. A wooden barrel held ramrods, and the

Duck hunting—two men and their catch. *Courtesy of the Georgetown County Museum.*

characteristic smell of gun oil and Hoppe's gun cleaning solvent hung over all. Along one wall were hooks holding miscellaneous generations of slickers, caps, cartridge cases and leather scabbards. The boots were ranged underneath—snake-proof Gokeys, lace-up jodhpur boots, knee-high riding boots and a rack of rubber Wellingtons and hip boots. Nothing was ever thrown away and we wore the same things for years.

I chose a brown canvas hat big enough so I could pull the brim down low over my forehead—"Never look up, the ducks can spy your white face a mile away!"—and pulled on my brother's old, leaky waders randomly patched with pink rubber squares. It was considered unnecessarily expensive to buy me a pair of my own. "You'll just grow out of them by next year." I fetched my shotgun, a 16-gauge Sauer that Daddy had given me for my twelfth birthday and we were off. I had taken the precaution of toasting a strawberry jam sandwich the night before, knowing from bitter experience that the duck hunt would last till my father had gotten his limit, no matter how cold it was or long it took or how hungry we became.

The paddle in the mysterious dark before dawn into the marsh in a flat-bottomed wooden duck boat is another never to be forgotten experience. The unsteady boat had about three inches of freeboard, and loose stems of marsh grass and corn shuck camouflage sloshed about in the bottom. I was in the bow and my father—not exactly skinny—balanced on the narrow middle seat. Wesley paddled silently and expertly from the stern, the stack of decoys piled in front of him. Invisible coots chuckled and rustled in the reeds, and occasionally a startled mallard flushed, rising up in the dark with a beating of wings and harsh, noisy quacking. Some mornings were so cold that the boatman had to crack the ice with his paddle before we could make it out to the blind in the middle of the pond. Wes carefully nudged the boat up to the narrow gap in the blind, we crawled awkwardly inside and he replaced the corn stalk "door."

After concealing us, he set about the strategic placement of the twenty or so wooden decoys, which were not the beautiful ones hand carved by the famous local hunter and guide, Huck Caines, but made by Mason Factory. Each decoy was painted to resemble a specific duck, and they were attached with green cord to little heavy weights so that they would bob just so in the shallow pond water.

The colder and more blustery the weather, the better the ducks got stirred up. My father hated a "blue bird day," but I can't say I minded too much. The ringnecks and teal would go ripping overhead, my shot following far behind. I almost never hit one because I couldn't seem to lead them far enough, or spot them coming in over the decoys in time to aim. "Mark!" he'd say, and then *SWOOSH!*—they'd come in low from behind the blind. *BANG!*—and my duck flared up and away, unscathed. I would have to sit there freezing until Daddy got his limit, and I was sure I would perish each time. After all, he could lean out of the blind to relieve himself, and I was trapped inside my canvas britches and layers of long underwear.

Another trouble I had was identifying the various ducks. They flew past in a blur, and technically each variety had its own bag limit. Luckily for them, I was such a bad shot that it didn't matter. It seemed as though my father could identify them from a mile away and choose the one he wanted. I don't remember what the limit was in the late 1930s, but it was nothing like the slaughter that went on at the turn of the century when two-hundred-duck days were bragged about over at Hobcaw Barony, Mr. Baruch's plantation, or Vanderbilt's Arcadia.

In other parts of the country, hunters use retrievers to swim out and bring back the wounded or dead ducks, but at our place my father thought that the danger from gators and water moccasins made swimming in the ponds too risky for our Labradors and spaniels who weren't kennel dogs, but part of the family. In the past, many gators were shot, and when cut open revealed grisly dog-collar mementos of fatal deer or coon hunts.

Captain Foster Bourne. South Island Plantation hunting by boat. *Courtesy of the Wright-Skinner family collection and the Georgetown County Museum.*

At the end of the hunt, the boatman paddled out and picked up the dead ducks. Some had floated into the reeds and it took a long while to find them. I always felt sorry for the waiting men, who had to crouch for hours on the edge of the rice field during those freezing mornings, marking where each duck went down. They built little fires while they waited patiently for the whistle that would signal my father's willingness to end the hunt—finally. From the blind you could see the tiny orange flames flickering away on the edge of the marsh.

One memorable morning an otter surged up and took a wounded, struggling duck off the water right in front of the blind, depriving Daddy of the evidence he needed to prove he had gotten his limit. But then, armed with that most unusual excuse, we at last went home to a big breakfast of grits and pancakes in our cozy dining room in front of the roaring fire.

The anxious wait in the blind for the first rushing flight of ducks that appears from nowhere, brings the same excitement today as it did in my own now distant youth, and the ducks are still just as hard to hit—harder

View of the rice fields with the ditch "trunk" for controlling the water level. *Courtesy of Frances Cheston Train.*

really—because there are far fewer in our area. Along the Atlantic flyway the construction boom has compromised the migration routes and the solid string of towns with night illumination confuse their traditional migratory paths. The federal limit has been greatly reduced—and rightly so—and today we no longer hunt duck at Friendfield. We would rather preserve them than eat them. The rice fields are now rest areas for the ever fewer migrating ducks, and the relentless proliferation of that invasive plant *Phragmites australis* has choked many of the ponds and further limited the number of ducks using our marsh.

By about 1900, rice was no longer grown commercially in the area. The crop had created enormous wealth for the Carolina planters in the days when they counted on intensive slave labor to plant and harvest. After the turn of the century, because of two devastating hurricanes in a row and the end of cheap labor, rice was not a commercially viable crop. The sticky, black mud called "pluff" bogged down oxen, mules and tractors. Only manpower—that is, black manpower—could work those once valuable rice fields. Today, most of the former rice fields have reverted to tidal marsh and federal law prohibits man-made construction in wetlands. Even hundred-year-old dikes and ditches cannot be repaired legally without reams of special permits.

River scene. *Courtesy of the Caledonia Plantation Collection and the Georgetown County Museum.*

A few years ago, an elderly, irascible plantation owner and friend of ours got so mad at a federal officer who ordered him to stop fixing up a breach in one of his dikes that he chased him off with a shotgun. I don't know what the outcome was. Southerners still passionately resent government interference of any kind.

Some rice for home consumption was raised on Friendfield until 1942. I remember when I was a child watching the plantation women using traditional techniques, flailing and winnowing the rice, near the old, sagging rice barn. Both it and the rice mill have since been torn down for safety's sake.

So, the rice culture is no more—killed off by the hurricanes at the beginning of the twentieth century, the end of slave labor and the unsuitability of machines to cope with the sticky, black pluff mud. In the Lowcountry rice has been replaced by the valuable timber crop, and now almost all of the old rice plantations have been consumed by condominiums, gated communities and golf courses. Traces of the old sweetness of life remain, but the flood of newcomers has diluted the essential South.

In my day, the men from that part of the South were all hunters, born and bred, brought up with a gun from the earliest age. Hunting and fishing were a way of life. The wives baked feather-light biscuits and cakes, participated in the church events and taught their daughters to be Southern ladies. It was all part of my childhood and I loved it—although I was much more of a tomboy than a "little lady." On vacations, when I was watching James or Tom skin a coon and learning not to be scared of snakes, my friends at home were going to parties, to museums and on ski trips.

Looking back, I wouldn't trade my experiences at Friendfield for anything, though when I was a teenager I remember staying awake on New Year's Eve, enviously listening to the countdown from Times Square on my radio and waiting for the ball to drop that traditionally ushered in the New Year. My mother and father had gone up to bed at nine-thirty as usual. "When you wake up, you'll be a whole year older," they said annually. This was no comfort at all for missing the fun I was sure that my friends were having at their parties.

As a youngster I was virtually unaware of the harsh realities emphasized by Charles Joyner in his book, *Down by the Riverside: A South Carolina Slave Community*, about the Gullah people of Johns Island, South Carolina:

> *The policy was called segregation, or Jim Crow. It was very thoroughgoing, and behind the mask of civility our harsh racial caste system branded all Black South Carolinians as inferior. Segregation was characterized by two sets of almost everything; one set of churches, stores, funeral homes, toilets, drinking fountains for black Carolinians, and another for white Carolinians. Black students were relegated to Jim Crow schools, black travelers to the back of the Jim Crow bus, black moviegoers to the Jim Crow balcony, and there were separate neighborhoods for blacks and whites. It was not difficult to tell which were which: the pavement ended where the black neighborhoods began. But not everything came in pairs. Some things such as parks, libraries and swimming pools were rarely available to black Carolinians at all.*

My own opinion, however, after much reflection, is that the hardships of Reconstruction, which gravely affected both blacks and whites, forged a common bond between the races in spite of these abuses. In the rural South today there still exists a courtesy and understanding between blacks and whites, which is rarely found in the Northern cities. The shared heritage of farming and hunting, the armed services and strong religious faith brought the races closer together. Although the civil rights movement created legal equality, and the problems of the past are lessening, troubles are by no means over. Education and jobs are the key to true racial equality. There is still de facto segregation today, although in the Georgetown Historical District, homes belonging to both races have shared the same streets since post–Civil War days.

Friendfield Plantation, its Southern culture and Lowcountry environment has created a lasting influence on me and my children and grandchildren. My family understands and deeply appreciates this powerful attachment. Country wisdom and colorful humor, the importance of family ties, courtesy, patriotism, the rewards of hard work and the love of nature have been its enduring gifts.

# Epilogue

So there they are, these memories of my happy and fortunate childhood, growing up in the 1930s. It was a childhood dominated by sentiment, by family, by well-loved houses, country environments and fun.

Afterward, off came the rose-colored glasses and the real life began. But that's another story.

Visit us at
www.historypress.net

www.ingramcontent.com/pod-product-compliance
Lightning Source LLC
Chambersburg PA
CBHW060807100426

42813CB00004B/983